THE LIBRARY
ST. MARY'S COLLEGE OF MARYLAND
ST. MARY'S CITY, MARYLAND 20686
W9-BKW-502

The Odyssey of New Religious Movements

Persecution, Struggle, Legitimation

A Case Study of the Unification Church

John T. Biermans

Symposium Series
Volume 19

The Edwin Mellen Press
Lewiston/Queenston

The Odyssey of New Religious Movements
Persecution, Struggle, Legitimation
A Case Study of the Unification Church

John T. Biermans

ISBN 0-88946-710-2
Copyright © 1986 by John T. Biermans

This is volume 19 in the continuing series
SYMPOSIUM SERIES
Volume 19 ISBN 0-88946-710-2
SS Series ISBN 0-88946-989-X

Cover design: David Hose

All rights reserved. For information contact

The Edwin Mellen Press
Box 450
Lewiston, New York
USA 14092

The Edwin Mellen Press
Box 67
Queenston, Ontario
L0S 1L0 CANADA

Printed in the United States of America

To My Parents

About the Author

John Biermans grew up on a farm in Southern Ontario, Canada. He studied political science at the University of Western Ontario (UWO) where he began his political career as Treasurer and later as President of the UWO Liberal Association. In 1974, he was elected Student Director of the Ontario Liberal Party. From 1974-1976 he served as special assistant and later executive assistant to Norman A. Cafik, Member of Parliament and Parliamentary Secretary to the Minister of Health and Welfare and later to the Minister of Consumer and Corporate Affairs in Ottawa.

Mr. Biermans studied law at the University of Toronto and the University of San Francisco, receiving his Juris Doctor degree in 1981. He is a practicing attorney admitted to the Bar of the State of New York. He is active in numerous legal associations including the American Bar Association and the New York County Lawyers Association.

He joined the Unification Church in 1977. He is married and the father of one daughter.

ACKNOWLEDGEMENTS

There are countless people who deserve special thanks for making this book possible. Without listing every person, I would like to thank Patrick Martin, Frank Flinn, Richard Jorandby, James Baughman, James Park, Herbert Richardson and Dean Kelley for their many insights and inspiration. For reviewing the manuscript and offering many helpful comments, I wish to thank Donald Jones, James Lewis, Lowell Streiker, Susan Henry, Dirk Antonis, Mose Durst, Donald Lunde, Michael Hertzberg, Al Sciarrino, Kaye Allen, David Hager, Kevin Smith, Joseph Fichter, Thomas McGowan, James Richardson, David Bromley, Robert Morton, Andrew Bacus, Michael Mickler, Frederick Sontag and Jonathan Gullery.

On a practical level, I am deeply appreciative to Louise Zontek and Marianne Colglazier for typing the manuscript as well as to the Edwin Mellen staff for all of their tremendous assistance in completing the book. To David Hose for his moral support and cover design, I owe special gratitude.

Those who sacrificed most while this book was written were my wife Hannelore and daughter Alicia. Without their wonderful support and understanding, I could not have accomplished this important work.

Finally, I wish to thank my spiritual guides who gave me new life and showed me how I could come to know God as a living reality in my life.

FOREWORD

by Dean M. Kelley

In this book John Biermans has made three important contributions. He has gathered together the pertinent findings of social science researchers and courts of law on the subject of new religious movements and the persecution they suffer. He has added the insights of his own personal experience as a member of the Unification Church who has been the victim of an unsuccessful attempt at "deprogramming." And he has included information from his files gathered as one of the staff attorneys of the Unification Church, recording the experience of other members at the hands of would-be faith-breakers.

These contributions are very much needed to counter the prevailing misinformation and hysteria about "cults" that have been so successfully spread by articulate anticultists and sensation-seeking media. The average person has little opportunity to survey the scholarly literature on this issue and so is unaware that most of it does not support the anticult hysteria, which is largely based on atrocity tales disseminated by apostates and equally unreliable allegations circulated by a handful of mental-health practitioners who appear to know very little about religion.

At the scholarly conferences of the Religious Research Association, the Society for the Scientific Study of Religion and the Association for the Sociology of Religion numerous research papers are presented on the various new religious movements by highly regarded observers like Gordon Melton, David Bromley, Anson Shupe, Tom Robbins, Dick Anthony, Eileen Barker, James Richardson, Herbert Richardson, the late William Shepherd, and many others (I mention these names because I happen to know these individuals and have respected their work over the years). They represent the prevailing consensus in the community of students of religious behavior, and that consensus views the anticultists' shrill denunciations as simply contrary to the general body of empirical evidence gathered by people who are not trying to foment a vendetta against "the cults."

It is, of course, quite possible that some individuals have had a bad experience with a particular new religious group at some particular time and place, just as there are individuals who have had a bad experience with one or another of the older and more conventional religions. But a few bad experiences do not necessarily discredit an entire category of organizations in other walks of life.

A similar common-sense perspective needs to be brought to the study of new religious movements, and John Biermans' sampling of the scholarly literature helps to restore perspective on that subject.

It is helpful, within that perspective, and contributing to it, to have the views of some "insiders," since outsiders alone, however objective or sympathetic, cannot fully interpret the experience of any religion. Insiders' accounts, taken alone, can of course be as misleading and self-serving on the one side as critics' and apostates' testimony on the other. But they provide a needed depth to the perspective that can be gained from no other source. In studying any social organization, particularly a religion, one needs to ask, "How do they see themselves?" One should not be content with that data alone, but one should certainly not omit it, lest the result be the kind of outsider's caricature that is typical of muckraking journalism and anticult polemic. In this book John Biermans combines an insider's insight with extensive quotations and references from scholarly research and court decisions, which together give a three-dimensional perspective of verisimilitude.

In a way it is a pity that such a book as this should be needed. It should not be necessary in a land that prides itself on esteem for religious liberty (at least in the abstract) to insist that members of new religious movements really are human beings entitled to as much respect for their religious choices as anyone else. But when there are organized alarmists and detractors with articulate spokespersons who have made lucrative careers out of denouncing and combatting "cults," then at least some countermeasures are needed. And those of us who cannot make careers out of countermeasures owe a debt of gratitude to the few, like John Biermans, who have taken time from more constructive endeavors to try to set the record straight.

It is even more remarkable that an entire chapter and more should be necessary to try to counter the bizarre but prevalent notion that there is some secret technique of "mind-control" or "brainwashing" or "coercive persuasion" that enables some sinister cult-leaders to gain total mastery over the wills of other persons without their consent. It should not require lengthy and scholarly argumentation to establish the absurdity of this notion, but apparently it does, and even then many will not be convinced, any more than the average inhabitants of Massachusetts Bay Colony in the seventeenth century could be disabused of the notions of demon-possession and witchcraft.

Even a moment's common-sense reflection should enable one to realize that if someone had perfected the art of enslaving others without the continuous application of physical coercion, he would have discovered a power for which tyrants and sorcerers have been seeking for centuries, and he would not need to confine his ambitions to the relatively rickety instrument of a religious movement but could take over the world. That the leaders of so-called "cults" have no such magical powers is apparent from the facts that their recruiting efforts are relatively ineffective and that the rate of slippage from attrition (defections without outside intervention) is incredibly high. In fact, there is nothing in the phenomenon that cannot be explained by the age-old practices of persuasion, peer-pressure and conversion, all practices shared by older religions, the media, commercial advertising and political propaganda, and all protected by the First Amendment of the U.S. Constitution.

Some may think that this book comes along after the worst is over and the dust has begun to settle. It is true that forcible deprogrammings are not as frequent as they were a few years ago, but they still occur. The three federal circuit courts of appeals that have ruled on the issue have found deprogrammers liable to their victims under the federal civil-rights law, and none have found the contrary. Spokespersons for the anticult movement assure us that deprogramming is crude and passé, *but it still goes on,* and it is still the greatest offense against religious liberty on this continent in the latter half of the twentieth century.

The anticult movement has now professed to narrow its target to "*destructive* cults"—a term not known to social-science research in religion—and to characterize its work as simply "cult awareness education." Nevertheless, anticultists show no greater insight into, or respect for, the choices young adults make in religion than before. They insist that they are not violating anyone's religious liberty; they are merely trying to prevent actual harm to unsuspecting and victimized converts. It is certainly not a violation of religious liberty to warn people about the supposed dangers of some or all new religious movements, or to try to persuade those who are their members to depart (so long as force or threat of force is not used), even if the information relied on is faulty or biased (which it often is). That, too, is protected by the First Amendment (with a few narrow exceptions such as slander, libel and defamation). And there may indeed be some "cults" that are "destructive," though it is hard to see how that term applies to the groups about which the anticultists are so exercised, which are generally rather well-meaning, idealistic bands of people trying to do what they think God requires.

It seems that what really distresses the anticultists is *conversion,* especially to religious movements that make high demands of their members for commitment of the whole self to a spiritual cause. Apparently a gradual and partial commitment to a mild and conventional faith is permissible, but a sudden conversion to a rigorous and alien life-style with requirements of total allegiance to the faith is not. But religious liberty includes the right "to *change* (one's) religion or belief" (Article 18 of the Universal Declaration of Human Rights), and to do so suddenly and totally, whether others like it or not. Cautions of prudence and circumspection are always in order. Everyone should "look before they leap," in religion as in other of life's ventures. But arbitrarily maligning new religions and impugning their motives is not in order—even if protected by the First Amendment—if one makes *any* claim to respect other people's religious liberty.

And applying to new religions a double standard, so that it is thought to be iniquitous for them to do what is permissible for other religions or for other human enterprises, is dishonest and pharisaical. For instance, the Scientologists were criticized for being "deceptive" and "underhanded" in buying property in Clearwater, Florida, under an assumed name when that is a standard practice in the real-estate business, followed in the same period in nearby Orlando by the Walt Disney organization in buying up property for the development of Disneyworld. Giving wholehearted and unswerving loyalty to one's employer or labor union or lodge or (traditional) religion is thought to be a laudable thing, but giving such loyalty to a new religious movement is seen to be somehow pernicious.

As John Biermans and the many authors he quotes suggest, much of the hysteria generated by the anticult alarmists is needless. Most of the new religious movements are *not* deleterious to their members and may indeed improve their life-situations. When they cease to meet their members' needs and interests, the members move on to other things without the need for personality-damaging outside intervention. If people could learn to respect the religious choices of their (adult) offspring and to retain some perspective and (uncommon) common sense about such matters, religious liberty would be in much better condition than it is today in the United States. This book should help contribute to that end.

Dean M. Kelley,
Director for Religious
and Civil Liberty,
The National
Council of Churches,
New York City,
September 1986.

CONTENTS

NEW YORK POST, FRIDAY, JULY 5, 1985

"I don't care if he's turned 'em all into Moonies! Just get him out of here before he calls a mass wedding!"

[Courtesy Paul (Bay) Rigby—New York Post.]

INTRODUCTION

The Unification Church is a contemporary religious movement with a comprehensive theology, philosophy and social theory. The movement was founded by Rev. Sun Myung Moon who was born in Korea, January 6, 1920. Initially a member of the Presbyterian Church, he officially founded the movement in 1954 in Seoul, Korea. It became established in the United States and spread through most of the world during the 1970's.

During that time, Rev. Moon and his missionaries seemed to stir up controversy everywhere they went. They manifested a zeal that was, at the very least, uncommon, if not downright bizarre to traditional religious sensibilities. There was the very strongly anti-communist teaching, the Oriental roots of the movement and, above all, the novel and somewhat revolutionary theology which more established denominations saw as a challenge. Those who became converts to the movement often made dramatic changes in their lifestyles, causing much concern and consternation to families and friends. In short, this new religious movement confronted the status quo of society on almost every level.

In order to find an explanation for this phenomenon, various concepts were formed by critics of the Church with the enthusiastic assistance of the media. People decided that the behavior of these converts to the Unification Church was highly unusual and unacceptable. They concluded that these young people must be under some form of mind control or hypnosis which caused them to work such long hours for this Korean "empire-builder." To some it was reminiscent of the attempt by the Chinese communists to brainwash American POW's during the Korean War—hence the term "brainwashing."

As this viewpoint was being instilled into the American consciousness, a small group of detractors of the Unification Church and other new religious movements began to take the situation into their own hands through a process of forcibly abducting adherents and holding them against their will (usually in exchange for an exorbitant fee from the adherent's parents) until they renounced their beliefs. This practice became know as "deprogramming" because of the contention by its practitioners that young converts had been "programmed" by Rev. Moon to the point that they were unable to exercise their own "free will", and that to "rescue" them, the process would have to be reversed.

"Deprogrammers" or, to be more precise, "faithbreakers" harvested a pool of embittered ex-members known as apostates. Their stories, like the ex-member tales against many religions throughout history, fanned the flames of hostility to the point that Rev. Moon and the Unification Church were harassed by numerous government agencies across the United States and elsewhere. One of these investigations led to tax evasion charges being filed against Rev. Moon in 1981. Despite a highly publicized appeal, which included wide-ranging support from the religious and civil liberties communities, Rev. Moon was jailed in July of 1984 and released in August of 1985.

In reality, the Unification Church is not the first new religious movement to encounter controversy, nor is it the first to be labelled a "cult" or "sect." The early Christians and the followers of St. Francis were considered to be "cults" by their contemporaries. The Unification Church stands in the very respectable company of what are now established religious denominations which initially experienced great controversy. Certainly Catholics, Baptists, Presbyterians, Methodists, Unitarians, Mennonites, Quakers, Jews, Mormons, Christian Scientists, Jehovah's Witnesses have experienced tremendous persecution at one time or another. To one who is uneducated in this unglorious history, it may seem that the controversy surrounding Rev. Moon and the Unification Church, particularly during the mid-to-late 1970's, was unique. But again, the hysterical allegations of "brainwashing" and "mind control" that have been leveled against the Unification Church are strongly reminiscent of what has been said about new or minority religious movements for thousands of years.

Despite the fact that much has been spoken and written about the Unification Church over the past 10-15 years, it is still necessary to ask how much the public really knows about this movement. What has been the source of the hostility? Are there factual bases for the charges and allegations that have been leveled against this church? Are "Moonies" really "brainwashed"? Is there such a thing as "brainwashing" at all? Does Rev. Moon really control every aspect of Unification Church members' lives? If the movement is so controversial why do people join? What is its appeal?

Over the past ten years, a great number of academic studies of the Unification Church have been carried out by scholars of many disciplines. Literally thousands of Unification Church members and former members have provided the raw data for these studies through interviews, questionnaires and participation in debates. The results have been published in scholarly periodicals, journals and books. Most of them, however, remain unknown to the general public.

This book will examine these key questions about the Church. It is an attempt to summarize and integrate many of the basic conclusions of the various studies in a coherent and analytic format. In effect, it will seek to set the record straight regarding the Unification Church (and new religions in general), to expose some of the myths that have been created and to offer useful insights into the dynamics of the religious experience in a secular world.

Chapter 1

RELIGIOUS BIGOTRY: AN HISTORICAL VIEW

Religious bigotry is nothing new. It has existed as long as religion has existed. History is replete with examples of this sad phenomenon from the persecution and enslavement of the Hebrews by Pharaoh to the attacks on religious "cults" of today.[1] Many people would agree that more death, injustice and human misery have been caused by religious bigotry and persecution than any other single cause.

The most shameful aspect of American history has been the mistreatment of racial and religious minorities, in contrast to the beautiful language of the United States Constitution and the Bill of Rights. Harvey Cox, Professor of Divinity at Harvard University, has written that:

> *Despite the elegant rhetoric about the Pilgrim fathers and the smiling exchanges at interfaith banquets, America has not set an exemplary record in the area of religious freedom. The English Calvinists who settled in Plymouth and Massachusetts Bay did not come to found a society where spiritual liberty would reign supreme. They came to found a theocracy....Unpopular and unconventional religious beliefs and practices were not only unwelcome, they were not tolerated. Roger Williams, a Baptist, was hounded into the frozen wilderness. When Henry Dunster, the president of Harvard College, decided not to have his fourth infant baptized because he had come to accept adult baptism, he was forced to retire. Later on, in other parts of the country, Mormons, Jews, Masons, Jesuits and ordinary Roman Catholics felt the hard edge of harassment and discrimination because of their religious convictions. A couple of generations ago, Jehovah's Witnesses were the main target of prejudice. Now we have the 'cults' It seems Americans are never really happy unless there is some unfamiliar religious group to abuse. The spirit of theocracy lingers on.*[2]

Defining the term 'cult'

Before going any further let us explore what is meant by the word 'cult.' Geoffrey Nelson states that "all founded religions can be seen as having developed from cults."[3] Jesuit sociologist Joseph Fichter suggests that the small group of original followers of Jesus constituted a Jewish cult that evolved over the years into a sect and eventually into a denomination.[4] Legal commentator Walter De Socio writes that "the term 'cult' is ambiguous, ill-defined and shrouded in both skepticism and mysticism. One man's path to Heaven is another man's subversive organization."[5] As Dean Kelley of the National Council of Churches explains, the word "cult" is simply a derogatory term for a religion we do not understand and don't like.[6] Two of America's leading experts on new religious movements, sociologists David Bromley and Anson Shupe, assert that the term "is a fashionable buzz word thrown about haphazardly by the media, anticultists, establishment ministers (who no longer worry about the label being applied to them), and even some social scientists who should know better."[7]

The great divergence in opinion as to what constitutes a "cult" is demonstrated by comparing the differing views of two organizations which are active in attacking the so-called "cults"— the Union of American Hebrew Congregations (UAHC) and the Spiritual Conterfeits Project. The former has vehemently attacked "Hebrew Christians" and "Jews for Jesus" as being among the most dangerous cults. Such groups are attacked for their alleged deception and for preying upon "people who are under emotional stress, who have various problems, are lonely, perhaps alienated, looking for answers."[8]

On the other hand, Brooks Alexander, a leader of the Berkeley, California Spiritual Counterfeits Project asserts that "Jews for Jesus" is not a cult:

> *In the first place the concept of "cult" should not be equated with the intensity of commitment or involvement which is characteristic of the so called high demand groups, religious or secular. Nor is aggressiveness or proselytizing cultish in itself. Both of these qualities—in one form or another—are basic to authentic Christianity...These two qualities in particular are worth singling out because they have apparently been*

the basis for mislabeling some groups as cults. Two groups which have occasionally been the target for such mistaken identification are "Jews for Jesus" and Campus Crusade for Christ.[9]

This lack of agreement and the arbitrariness of the "cult" label is evident in the following remarks by Legislator Breaugh during a debate in the Legislature of the Province of Ontario, Canada, about a proposed bill dealing with the "cultists":

I know people, friends of mine, who did what I thought were irrational acts when they were 16 and 17 years of age. They went off to convents and seminaries. They renounced worldly goods. They took a vow of poverty. They gave up the automobiles and the hockey sticks and the football games that I wanted and thought were important. They didn't want to go out with girls. They wanted to go into a seminary. How strange, I thought. How can they do that?

They wore funny clothes. They had values the rest of the society didn't have. Were they a cult? No, they were Jesuits. I think, quite frankly, the Jesuit order in Canada and in the world has proved its value to our society.[10]

Historical Examples of Religious Bigotry

Many researchers and scholars have compared present-day attacks on the religious "cults" to numerous other periods when persecution was in vogue against one religion or another. Charges of satanic possession and brainwashing have repeatedly been made against unpopular religions. There is the myth of the "evil eye," the notion that under an evil and designing influence, one will reject traditional religious beliefs in favor of unfamiliar ones. As Harvey Cox notes, brainwashing is simply a "more psychologically acceptable way of expressing what was expressed previously in other ways. The brainwashing version of the evil eye myth holds that 'these people' are the victims of prophets, spell-binders, witches or hypnotists."[11]

David Bromley and Anson Shupe have drawn parallels between the allegations of detractors of new religious movements (better known as "anti-cultists") such as Robert Lifton, John Clark and Margaret Singer[12] to the persecution of witches in 17th century America. Witches, according to their accusers, had supposedly been inveigled into mortal sin by the Tempter's diabolical skills. Witches were said to bear identifiable stigmata of their demonic possession such as radical distortion of vocal qualities, speech patterns reflecting the will of the demon rather than the victim, nervous agitation, an ashen pallor; they were said to be "blerie-eyed," "hunch-backed," hollow-eyed, and afflicted with "fowle odours."[13] It was also said that all of these signs would suddenly vanish when the victim was "exorcised" and returned to his "normal" condition. Likewise, members of modern day religious "cults" are routinely accused by their detractors of being mindless "zombies."

Herbert Richardson, professor of theology at the University of Toronto, expands on this analogy between the allegations of brainwashing of today and the accusations that certain people were "bewitched" during the period between the fourteenth and the seventeenth centuries. He points out that the illness of "being bewitched" was acutally "created" by "scientific" specialists during this time.[14] In colonial America, the most prominent of the witch-hunters was Cotton Mather, a leading Puritan minister, who carried out witchcraft investigations in Salem, Massachusetts. As evidence he would cite a series of outrageous accusations. For instance, in the Trial of Martha Carrier in Salem, August 2, 1692 he stated that:

> *Martha Carrier was indicted for the bewitching of certain persons, according to the form usual in such cases, pleading NOT GUILTY to her Indictment; there were first brought in a considerable number of the bewitched persons who not only made the court sensible of a horrid Witchcraft committed upon them, but also deposed that it was Martha Carrier, or her shape, that grievously tormented them by biting, pricking, pinching, and choking of them....Moreover, the look of Carrier laid the afflicted people for dead; and her touch, if her eye at the same time were off them; raised them again....*[15]

After hearing these and similar evidences of her witchcraft, the court concluded that Martha Carrier was a witch and burned her to death.[16]

The noted church-and-state scholar Leo Pfeffer writes that in one Salem case all twelve of the jurors subsequently signed a statement admitting their error in handing down guilty verdicts. Of the defendants in other jury trials (involving several hundred young women and "afflicted children"), nineteen were hanged.[17] In Europe the witch hunts were even worse with many thousands being executed.

The attacks on the Roman Catholic Church in America have been some of the most blatant expressions of religious bigotry. Catholics were popularly and derogatorily called "Papists" throughout the Colonies (even in Maryland which was founded by Catholics). Typical of the discrimination was a 1647 decree by the General Court of Massachusetts that: "No Jesuit or ecclesiastical person ordained by the Pope or the see of Rome shall henceforth come into Massachusetts. Any person not freeing himself of suspicion shall be jailed, then banished. If taken a second time he shall be put to death."[18] Anti-Catholic feeling ran so high that most colonies at one time or another enacted anti-Catholic legislation.[19]

During the 19th century, a nativist party known as the "Know-Nothing" Party became active and captured control of the legislatures in a number of states. Its stated purpose was "Anti-Romanism, Anti-Bedinism, Anti-Pope's Toeism, Anti-Nunnerism, Anti-Winking Virginism, Anti-Jesuitisim, and Anti-the-Whole-Sacerdotal Hierarchism with all its humbugging mummeries."[20]

In an action somewhat parallel to the many investigations of the Unification Church, the "Know-Nothing" Legislature in Massachusetts appointed a "Nunnery Committee" to report on "such theological seminaries, boarding schools, academies, nunneries, convents, and other institutions of like character as they may deem necessary."[21] Leo Pfeffer explains that this reflected a widely-held "belief that young women did not voluntarily commit themselves to serving their religion as nuns but were the victims of physical duress or 'mind-control' (a belief reflected today in a practically universal assumption respecting 'cults')." He adds: "There was, indeed, strong condemnation of convents on the ground that unlawful means were supposedly used to force young women into them."[22]

These accusations seemed to find total verification by the likes of Maria Monk, Rebecca Reed, Edith O'Gorman and Sister Ligouri, who were apostates from their faith. In her outrageous book, *Awful Disclosures of the Hotel Dieu Nunnery of Montreal,* first published in 1836 and frequently reprinted, Maria Monk claimed to be an ex-member of a convent where, she alleged, Catholic nuns were "executed for refusing to obey the lustful will of priests."[23] She also claimed that she had become pregnant by a priest and that she had to escape because she would have had to strangle her infant at birth. In his highly regarded book *The Protestant Crusade 1800-1860,* Ray Billington exposes the background of the Maria Monk story as did noted historian Sydney Ahlstrom in his book *A Religious History of the American People.* Both Billington and Ahlstrom state that this vicious fiction was the work of several anti-Catholic clergymen who did most of the writing of the book.[24]

Another ex-nun, Rebecca Reed, told stories of her "captivity" that were so inflammatory that a Protestant mob burned her former convent to the ground.[25] Yet another, Edith O'Gorman, pleaded that "the legislature enact laws for the inspection of convents." She implored, "Let the prison doors of monasteries and convents be thrown open to their deluded inmates."[26]

England was also swept by this tide of anti-Catholic feeling during the late 19th century[27] and it spread to other members of the Commonwealth, including Australia. In a case comparable to Maria Monk, "Sister Ligouri," an Irish-born nun who "escaped" from her convent at Wagga in Australia and was promoted enthusiastically by the Loyal Orange Order, became a "cause celebre." Australian researcher Gregory Tillett marvels at the "sensationalist stories of life 'behind convent walls,' 'brainwashing,' seduction (both spiritual and physical) of innocent children by sinister priests, vast sums of money being collected for the 'foreign' Pope, bizarre rituals and inhuman disciplines." He adds that if one simply changed the period and changed the names, these could be stories run by the popular press as reports about the Unification Church and other new religious movements today.[28]

The Baptists have also experienced severe persecution during their history. In 1635, Roger Williams was exiled from his home in Boston by the general Court of Massachusetts. He fled to Rhode Island where he formed the first Baptist church in America. This was the beginning of the Baptist crusade to protect religious freedom, a cause that frequently led to intense persecution. Church-and-state attorney Lee Boothby, who serves as general counsel to the Americans United for Separation of Church and State, writes:

> *Because the Baptists were champions for the cause of church-state separation and religious liberty as opposed to the established Anglican Church in pre-revolutionary America, particularly in Virginia, they were victims of great oppression and persecution by that colony. Baptist clerics were arrested, fined, whipped, and imprisoned ostensibly for disturbing the peace, but the punishment really resulted from the preaching of their faith. Baptists were also victimized by the laws requiring church attendance at the established church.*[29]

This was reminiscent of the terrible persecution experienced by the Anabaptists (who were the forerunners of such groups as the Quakers and the Mennonites) throughout Europe at the hands of both Catholics and Protestants during the 16th century. Despite severe abuse, the Anabaptists persisted in evangelizing among the established churches. They paid a heavy price for their converts as theologian Franklin Littell of Temple University explains:

> *Martyrdom was the carrying power of the movement, the triumph beyond obvious defeat, the final long pilgrimage free from the world and its controls....The Anabaptists knew what it was to invite new members to "take up their cross." In this trial by fire and water and the sword, where their faith was tested as gold in the furnace, they were fortified by the memory of Christ's suffering and by the hymns and records of other brethren of the cross. The first hymns were from prison, and the finest records were stories of the martyrs who "have sealed in knightly fashion the truth of God with their blood."*[30]

In a book entitled *The Quiet Rebels,* Margaret Bacon documents the terrible abuse suffered by the Quakers in the Massachusetts Bay colony during the mid-1600's. They were arrested, whipped, committed to the House of Corrections, kept constantly at work and prevented from conversing with anyone.[31] In some instances, Quakers were held in solitary confinement while others, such as Mary Dyer, were executed in the Boston Common. Dyer was hung for the simple reason that she refused to stop witnessing and testifying to her faith. Today she stands as a symbol for religious liberty.[32]

The severe persecution of the Mormons and the murder of their prophet Joseph Smith in 1844 were further incidents that blot the record of American history. Harvey Cox writes: "There is voluminous literature about how all of the Mormon women were being kept captive in polygamy by the brutal charismatic charm of the Mormon leaders. According to this material, there were no women living in Salt lake City in the middle of the nineteenth century who were there voluntarily."[33]

During a 1984 hearing on religious liberty by the Senate Subcommittee on the Constitution, its Chairman, Senator Orrin Hatch, himslf a Mormon, remarked: "I happen to belong to the only church in the history of this country that had an extermination order put out against its members by a state governor."[34]

The persecution of the Jewish people has been perhaps the most tragic aspect of human history. The Jewish people have borne the brunt of the bigotry of the world for centuries. The Holocaust of Hitler's Germany was the culmination of many, many years of abuse and propaganda. Certainly the publication of the infamous *Protocols of the Elders of Zion* played a significant role in fanning the flames of anti-Semitism in the years before and after the turn of the last century. This fabricated document, which was supposedly written by leading Jews in Tsarist Russia at the turn of the last century, was, in fact, created to spread disinformation about the Jewish people. Samuel Katz, a leading Israeli government official during the 1970's, states that this book "has long been a central pillar of the vast edifice of anti-Semitic indoctrination." He adds that to a large extent, "the *Protocols* provided the ideological justification for the physical destruction of the Jewish peole. It was employed in Tsarist Russian anti-Semitism, it was one of the textbooks of German Nazism, and it has been called the "father of the Holocaust."[35]

Katz writes that even today Arab teenagers are taught about *The Protocols of the Elders of Zion* "as a factual work, a Jewish admission of the conspiracy to dominate the world."[36] Anti-Semitism is also a frequent theme in contemporary Soviet literature. Common expressions are "Zionist bankers...Zionist monopolies...the Jewish faction of the world oligarchy...." Sovietologist Albert Weeks suggests that in recent decades "Kremlin propaganda has sounded more and more like an echo of the pages of the *Protocols*."[37]

Gordon Allport, one of the leading social psychologists of this century, discusses the residual anti-Semitism in the United States in his classic work, *The Nature of Prejudice*. His research shows that at least ten percent of the population had virulent feelings of antagonism towards Jewish people, with some research showing as much as fifty percent holding at least a mild anti-Jewish feeling.[38] In particular, Allport notes the anti-Semitism among some Christian clergy. By way of example, he includes the following excerpts from one clergyman's sermon:

> *The synagogue is worse than a brothel...it is the den of scoundrels...It is a criminal assembly of Jews...a place of meeting for the assassins of Christ...a den of thieves; a house of ill fame, a dwelling of iniquity....I would say the same things about their souls....Debauchery and drunkenness have brought them to the level of the lusty goat and the pig....We should not even salute them, or have the slightest converse with them....They are lustful, rapacious, greedy, perfidious robbers.*[39]

It was this sort of outrageous bigotry that led to the persecution of the Jewish people in America—a bigotry that many feel still lingers today.[40]

Donald E. Miller, Chairman of the Department of Religion at the University of Southern California wrote that the utopian groups in America during the nineteenth century were almost all subjected to continual harassment for their supposedly deviant beliefs and practices. The late nineteenth century saw the eruption of anti-Semitism with the emigration of Jews to America. Quakers faced the death sentence (later commuted) for their refusal to bear arms. The Jehovah's Witnesses evoked even greater hysteria leading to such persecutions as castration, burning of property, and other hostile acts.[41]

Comparing Past Persecution to the Present Day

In an article entitled "Deprogramming in Historical Perspective," Miller compares this historical experience to that of the new religious movements in recent years. He asserts that the pattern of response by the dominant culture to new religious movements is remarkably uniform. Bromley and Shupe who have done extensive study of new religions, particularly the Unification Church, echo this view: "As even a cursory review of American history reveals, virtually every major denomination and religious body was met initially with some degree of skepticism, ostracism or persecution. Indeed, the parallels with contemporary religious groups are striking."[42]

Miller explains that it is common to cast into question the leaders of a new religious movement by attacking their character and motives. Routinely, charges are made of sexual, legal and financial misconduct. The membership itself is commonly accused of engaging in sexually licentious behaviour or other cruel, inhumane or indecent activity. Furthermore, new religions are often portrayed as a political threat because of ideology or origin in a foreign country. Finally, Miller argues, the process of education and recruitment of new members is labeled "as 'brainwashing,' hence evoking the sympathy of the 'objective' outsider to the plight of the helpless."[43]

This resembles the analysis of Harvey Cox in his article "Myths Sanctioning Religious Persecution." Cox points out that witches were alleged to have sexual intercourse with Satan. The Amish were said to engage in similar activities in their barns, and there is the recurrent story of the "tunnel connecting the priests' residence to the convent."[44] Cox adds:

> *The rumors suggest mouth-watering sexual excesses, midnight orgies, and other delectations forbidden to the conventional populace....It is astonishing how often this theme recurs through the centuries. The early Christians were accused of, and widely believed to engage in, the eating of flesh and the drinking of blood....Medieval Jews were believed to kidnap and cannibalize young Christian children.*[45]

As for the presumed political threat of groups such as the Unification Church, Cox notes that this is also a recurring theme. Methodists were thought by the Anglicans to be spies during the 18th century. Baptists and Quakers were excluded from the Massachusetts Bay colony because they were perceived as a threat to the established state church. Cox adds that the magistrates in Massachusetts did not seem to know or care what the Quakers thought. "We hear of no record of what the Quakers were teaching. The fact that they refused to doff their hats in the presence of magistrates and governors seems to have been sufficient evidence that they were Quakers and, therefore, Quakers were a threat to public order."[46]

In many countries Catholics have continued to suffer on this account as well. It was believed that they could not be trusted because their loyalty was always first and foremost to the Pope in Rome. This was a charge that appeared again as late as 1960, during John F. Kennedy's campaign for the presidency. Cox writes:

> *Hence, anything they might say was intrinsically suspect because Catholics were permitted not to tell the truth when there was a conflict of loyalties. The same superstition used to be attached to Jews, who were believed to be absolved of all promises made during the year when they recited the Kol Nidre on the Day of Atonement. Perhaps the best example is that of the Jesuits, who were taught, so the myth goes, the principle of mental reservation. This meant that Jesuits could consciously lie, deceive, and distort whenever they thought some higher truth was to be served.*[47]

This allegation of deception is one of the most commonly raised critiques of new religious movements. After acknowledging the longstanding allegations of deception by the Jesuits, Father Joseph Fichter, a Jesuit himself, compares the charge of "heavenly deception" made against the Unification Church and other groups to the age-old rivalry between peoples of different religions:

> *Before the present era of ecumenical goodwill and interfaith understanding, the Jew who became a Christian was obviously coerced to do so. The young Protestant who converted to Catholicism was certainly bewitched by the wiles and deceptions of Rome. The so-called 'fallen away' Catholic who joined a Protestant Church had come under some evil influence that prevented him from thinking clearly. Ecumenism now absolves the switching of members among the large scale American religions; the charge of brainwashing is brought only when people are 'victimized' and 'tricked' into joining some new religious cult, especially one with an Oriental flavor.*[48]

As this brief overview of religious history attests, it is no disgrace for a religious movement to encounter persecution. In fact, some would argue that if a religious movement is not encountering resistance and opposition, it is not truly fulfilling its prophetic role. The prophet, the saint and the evangelist have traditionally come to challenge the lethargy of the established order.[49] They bring revival, renewal and reawakening to those who have ears to hear that the ways of the secular world are not God's ways. As the following chapters will demonstrate, Rev. Moon and the Unification Church can be seen to follow in this tradition. The resistance and opposition faced by the Unification movement during its short history bear a remarkable similarity to the abuse and persecution of religions throughout history.

References

1. The term "cult" is not used here to imply any endorsement of its negative connotation. It is used here for convenience only. Whenever possible, the term "new religious movements" will be used instead. See definitions of the term "cult" in the following pages.

2. See introduction to David G. Bromley and Anson D. Shupe, Jr., *Strange Gods: The Great American Cult Scare* (Boston: Beacon Press, 1981) xi. See also 211.

3. Joseph H. Fichter, *The Holy Family of Father Moon* (Kansas City: Leaven, 1985) 9. See also John A. Saliba, "Learning From The New Religious Movements," *Thought, Fordham University Quarterly,* Vol. LXI, June 1986, 227.

4. Ibid., 9-10. See also Kenneth Scott Latourette, *A History of Christianity* (New York: Harper, 1953) 23-24. In an earlier article, Father Fichter wrote that the Unification Church has "grown beyond the boundaries of the cult" and is "now a fully organized church with a scripture and a hierarchy." Fichter added that the Unification Church comprises "the four basic elements that social scientists declare essential ingredients of a religion: a belief system, a code of moral behavior, a pattern of worship and prayer, and a social structure. From this perspective the prediction of Frederick Sontag has already come true when he saw 'the movement inevitably evolving into another established church.'" See Joseph H. Fichter "Home Church: Alternative Parish" in Joseph H. Fichter (ed.), *Alternatives to American Mainline Churches* (New York: Rose of Sharon Press, 1983) 179.

5. Walter G. De Socio, "Protecting the Rights of Religious Cults," *Human Rights,* Vol. 8, Number 3, 1979, 38.

6. Fichter, *Holy Family of Father Moon,* supra, 10. Psychiatrist Joel Fort adds a similar view: "If someone belongs to a group we disapprove of, we call it a cult or worse; when we disagree and have difficulty understanding why someone maintains certain views that disagree with the norm or what we expect, we say they have been brainwashed." Joel Fort, "Mind Control: The What and How of Conversion and Indoctrination ('Brainwashing')" in H. Wang (ed.), *Clinical Hypnosis in Medicine* (Chicago: Yearbook Medical Publishers, 1981) 220.

7. Bromley and Shupe, supra, 21-22. See also Robert Ellwood, "The Several Meanings of *Cult,*" *Thought, Fordham University Quarterly,* vol. LXI, June, 1986, 212.

8. Herbert Richardson (ed.), *New Religions and Mental Health* (New York: Edwin Mellen, 1980) xii.

9. Ibid., xii, quoting Brooks Alexander, "What is a Cult," *Spiritual Counterfeits Newsletter,* v/i (Jan.-Feb., 1979).

10. *Legislature of Ontario Debates: Official Report* (Hansard), Fourth Session, 31st Parliament (Thursday, March 27, 1980, After Sitting) 284.

11. Cox, "Deep Structures in the Study of New Religions," in Jacob Needleman and George Baker (eds.), *Understanding the New Religions* (New York: Seabury, 1978) 122,127.

12. The significance of these three individuals will be explained in Chapters 2 and 3.

13. See Anson D. Shupe, Jr. and David G. Bromley, "Witches, Moonies, and Accusations of Evil" in Thomas Robbins and Dick Anthony (eds.), *In Gods We Trust; New Patterns of Religious Pluralism in America* (New York, Transaction Books, 1981).

14. Herbert Richardson, supra, xvi-xvii.

15. Cotton Mather, *On Witchcraft* (New York: Bell, 1974) 125-126.

16. Herbert Richardson, supra, xvii.

17. Leo Pfeffer, Brief Amicus Curiae for the Institute for the Study of American Religion, in support of petition for certiorari, Supreme Court of the United States, *Sun Myung Moon v. U.S.*, in Herbert Richardson (ed.), *Constitutional Issues in the Case of Reverend Moon* (New York: Edwin Mellen, 1984) 530, citing I.A. Stokes, *Church and State in the United States* (1960) 169-70.

18. Ibid., quoting Sanford H. Cobb, *The Rise of Religious Liberty in America* (New York: Macmillan, 1902) 177.

19. Ray Billington, *The Protestant Crusade 1800-1860,* (Chicago: Quadrangle, 1938) 9. See also Sydney E. Ahlstrom, *A Religious History of the American People* (New Haven: Yale University Press, 1972) 558-68.

20. Anson Phelps Stokes and Leo Pfeffer, *Church and State in the United States* (New York: Harper & Row, 1964) 236.

21. Ibid., 237. The comparable investigations of the Unification Church will be discussed in Chapter 8.

22. Pfeffer, ibid., 533.

23. Billington, supra, 99-100.

24. Ibid. See also Ahlstrom, supra.

25. Billington, supra, 71.

26. Edith O'Gorman, *Convent Life Unveiled* (London: Lile and Fawcett, circa 1881) 131.

27. A whole genre of Protestant literature developed in England in which horrific allegations were made against Roman Catholic orders: among them were Maria Ayesha, *The Truth about a Nunnery* (London: Chatto and Windus, 1912); William Hogan, *Auricular Confession and Popish Nunneries* (London: Dyer, 1846); W. Lancelot Holland, *Nuns Walled Up and Nuns*

Walled In (Edinburgh, 1895); Charlotte Myhill, *How Perversions are Effected, or Three Years' Experience as a Nun* (London: Walbrook, 1874).

28. Gregory Tillett, "The Moonies, The Media and Religious Persecution," (Unpublished) 1982, 6; citing "The Fate of Sister Ligouri," *The Sydney Morning Herald* (Sydney, Australia), July 19, 1889, 14.

29. Lee Boothby, "Government as an Instrument of Retribution for Private Resentments" in Dean Kelley (ed.), *Government Intervention in Religious Affairs II* (New York: Pilgrim Press, 1986) 81.

30. Franklin H. Littell, *The Origins of Sectarian Protestantism* (New York: Macmillan, 1964) 131.

31. Margaret H. Bacon, *The Quiet Rebels* (New York: Basic Books, 1969) 29.

32. Ibid., 33.

33. Cox, "Deep Structures," supra, 127.

34. Hearing Before the Senate Subcommittee on the Constitution, "Oversight on the State of Religious Liberty in America Today" 98th Cong. 2nd Sess. June 26, 1984, 3.

35. Samuel Katz, *Battleground* (New York: Bantam, 1973) 181. For a detailed explanation of the Protocols, see Norman R. Cohn, *Warrant for Genocide: The Myth of the Jewish World-Conspiracy and the Protocols of the Elders of Zion* (Chico, CA: Scholars Press, 1981).

36. Ibid., 183.

37. "A Whirlwind of Anti-Semitism Lies at Communism's Center," *New York City Tribune* (New York, N.Y.) July 23, 1986, 7.

38. Gordon W. Allport, *The Nature of Prejudice* (Reading, MA: Addison-Wesley, 1954) 74-75.

39. Ibid., 447-448, quoting from M. Hay, *The Foot of Pride* (Boston: Beacon Press, 1950) 26-32.

40. See, for example, a recent headline in the *New York Times*, "Yale's Limit on Jewish Enrollment Lasted Until Early 1960's, Book Says," *New York Times* (New York, N.Y.) March 4, 1986, Bl.

41. Donald E. Miller, "Deprogramming in Historical Perspective" in D. Bromley & J. Richardson (eds.), *The Brainwashing/Deprogramming Controversy* (New York: Edwin Mellen, 1983) 15.

42. David G. Bromley and Anson D. Shupe, Jr., "The Tnevnoc Cult," *Sociological Analysis*, Vol. 40, 1979, 361, 365.

43. Miller, ibid., 27.

44. H. Cox, "Myths Sanctioning Religious Persecution" in M. Darrol Bryant and Herbert Richardson (eds.), *A Time for Consideration* (New York: Edwin Mellen, 1978) 8.

45. Ibid., 7.

46. Ibid., 6.

47. Ibid., 9.

48. Joseph H. Fichter, "Youth in Search of the Sacred," in Bryan Wilson (ed.), *The Social Impact of New Religious Movements* (New York: Rose of Sharon Press, 1981) 29.

49. Paul E. Johnson, *Psychology of Religion* (Nashville: Abingdon, 1959). 180.

Chapter 2

THE BRAINWASHING MYTH

The charge that Unification Church members are "brainwashed" has perhaps been the most widely publicized allegation against the Church. Where did this theory come from and what does it mean?

Origins of the Theory

The concept of "brainwashing" originated as an attempt to explain what took place in prisoner-of-war camps during the Korean War. American soldiers were subjected to attempts by the Communists to change their political ideas about communism and capitalism through various deprivations, group discussions and written confessions. This, of course, was done while they were being held under total physical coercion. As a result, during captivity, some gave the appearance of having been changed, but only a few were genuinely changed in their political views.[1]

The term itself was coined by the English newspaperman Edward Hunter in 1951 to translate the Chinese phrase *Hsi nao* (literally "wash brain") which in Confucianism traditionally means to "purify one's thoughts." The more technical Chinese phrase is *szu-hsiang-kai-tsao* (literally, "thought-reconsider-change-previous") which has been variously labeled as "ideological remolding," "ideological reform" or "thought reform" by Robert Jay Lifton in *Thought Reform and the Psychology of Totalism, A Study of "Brainwashing" in China.*[2] Lifton in the same work warns that the loose usage of the term "brainwashing" makes "...the word a rallying point for fear, resentment, urges toward submission, justification for failure, irresponsible accusation, and for a wide gamut of emotional extremism."[3]

In Chapter 22 of *Thought Reform and the Psychology of Totalism,* Lifton sets out a list of categories, which, according to him, describe the methods of political re-indoctrination used by the Chinese after their victory in 1949. The following are Lifton's categories of "totalism" in their order of occurrence:

Milieu Control
Mystical Manipulation
The Demand of Purity
The Cult of Confession
The "Sacred Science"
Loading the Language
Doctrine Over Person
The Dispensing of Existence[4]

Deprogrammers and anti-cult organizations took over these *political* categories from the Chinese communist experience and applied them uncritically to the new religions without carrying out research on them, thereby creating a novel psycho-political stereotype. Furthermore, this analogy was made despite the lack of evidence that these religions engaged in the physical coercion so essential to the Communist practice.[5] Lifton himself gives occasion for this misapplication of Chapter 22 in his further discussion in the subsequent chapter where he states that "thought reform bears many resemblences to practices of organized religion."[6] Lifton's recent article, "Cult Processes, Religious Totalism, and Civil Liberties," essentially confirms his views on totalism in religious organizations.[7]

According to Lifton's notorious Chapter 22, there is a minimization of external influences, the development of special language and especially the manipulation of the recruit's sense of guilt. Lifton argues that inner doubts about even the most bizarre cult doctrine and practice are then attributed to one's own evil or the influence of the devil, as represented by society outside. Control over individual guilt, he asserts, is perpetuated by a variety of small and large group meetings, stressing criticism, self-criticism, continuous confession and, at times, public humiliation of those who appear to deviate. Attorney Robert N. Shapiro, on the other hand, points out that what Lifton fails to mention is that emphasis on individual guilt through the doctines of sin and damnation has always existed in established churches. He adds that Lifton also ignores "the guilt-based work ethic on which so much of secular society depends."[8]

Theologian Herbert Richardson, in an article entitled "Mental Health, Conversion and the Law," asserts that Lifton and others are making the claim that they have discovered a new form of mental illness. By way of example, Richardson describes the views of psychiatrist John Clark, who claims that ordinary methods of psychiatric diagnosis cannot adequately diagnose the condition of "brainwashing." According to Clark, the mental illness of being brainwashed is so subtle that it can elude an ordinary diagnosis. Hence, a brainwashed person may appear, to the ordinary psychiatrist, as perfectly normal and healthy. Clark argues that this only shows the depth and dangerousness of the condition—for the brainwashed person can actually fool an ordinary psychiatrist into thinking he is normal.[9]

Brainwashing Theory Repeatedly Discredited

Despite the emotional appeal of such charges, the brainwashing theory has been repeatedly discredited and dismissed by a wide variety of sociologists, psychiatrists, theologians and others. Psychiatrist Thomas Szasz of the State University of New York in Syracuse says simply that no one can "wash brains." Instead, "brainwashing" like many dramatic terms, is a "metaphor." He adds:

> *A person can no more wash another's brain with coercion or conversation than he can make him bleed with a cutting remark. If there is no such thing as brainwashing, what does this metaphor stand for? It stands for one of the most universal human experiences and events, namely, for one person influencing another. However, we do not call all types of personal or psychological influence "brainwashing." We reserve this term for influence of which we disapprove.*[10]

In his book *Mind-Bending,* religious counselor Lowell Streiker writes that he is "in total agreement" with Dr. Szasz.[11] He points out that the term brainwashing has been used loosely in many contexts such as "when people are upset with one another's stubbornness." He notes that the term has been used by critics to attack Billy Graham, Oral Roberts, Campus Crusade for Christ, tent evangelists, and so on. These evangelists are known for their ability to make people feel uncomfortable with their own way of life and for suggesting change.[12]

Streiker argues that these techniques are not mysterious. In fact, they have been used for centuries by "salesmen, politicians, prophets, and pimps." Streiker adds that "brainwashing" is simply a term of opprobrium, which indicates that someone does not approve of the consequences of a particular process. "Conversion" and "reform" are terms which indicate the speaker's approval of the results."[13]

Theologian Harvey Cox makes precisely this point when he states: "The term 'brainwashing' has no respectable standing in scientific or psychiatric circles, and it used almost entirely to describe a process by which somebody has arrived at convictions that I do not agree with."[14]

Dr. Walter Reich, a psychiatrist with the National Institute of Mental Health, aptly notes: "Psychiatry endangers itself—debases its coinage—by entering areas in which it lacks a broad base expertise. In [brainwashing] cases, psychiatric experience is limited and not widely tested. It does not amount to legal expertise."[15]

Thomas Robbins, a sociologist of religion, and Dick Anthony, a psychologist of religion, in their book *In Gods We Trust* add that Lifton's theory of equating various religions with prisoner-of-war camps is rather "far-fetched." They reach this conclusion in light of their findings that a significant number of people leave the Unification Church and other groups voluntarily and that a low percentage of those who attend religious seminars actually ever join such movements.[16]

This view, in regard to the Unification Church, is affirmed by many others, such as two Stanford psychiatrists Donald T. Lunde and Henry A. Sigal. From personal investigation at Unification Church retreats and interviews with current members as well as "bitter defectors," they reject Lifton's thesis. In particular, they note the absence of physical coercion or confinement at Unification Church facilities, both of which are necessary elements for the application of Lifton's theory.[17]

This factor has also been emphasized by Gene James, philosophy professor at Memphis State University, and British sociologist Eileen Barker. In a rather thorough study of the issue entitled "Brainwashing: The Myth and The Actuality," James points out that the "first and most obvious component of brainwashing as practiced by the Chinese (although its importance is sometimes ignored) is that it took place under conditions of imprisonment."[18] He asserts that the recruiting practices of new religions "are quite unlike brainwashing."[19]

In citing the allegations of similarity between the indoctrination methods employed by the Chinese and North Korean communists and the Unification Church, Eileen Barker suggests that such a comparison is highly suspect. She writes: "The trouble with this comparison would seem, *prima facie,* to be that an undeniable element of such practices was that the victims *were* prisoners (and that they were frequently subjected to physical torture). If the evidence shows that Moonies do not hold their guests as prisoners, let alone torture them, would not this suggest that such comparisons are beside the point?"[20]

It is worth noting here that Dr. Lunde and others [21] criticize the detractors of new religious movements for their failure to conduct complete investigations of the organizations they so roundly condemn.[22] Many of the most vocal anti-cult spokesmen refuse to conduct personal investigation of "cult" facilities. Margaret Singer, John Clark and Louis Jolyn West, for example, have never requested interviews with Unification Church leaders or asked to inspect church facilities. It appears that they are afraid of being "trapped" or "beguiled" by the church, as evidenced by West's critique of those who have conducted such investigations. West describes them as "apologists" who "appear to have been successfully gulled by charismatic cult leaders or their representatives. Some declare that they have visited a cult and been impressed by what they saw."[23] It might be that West refuses to "visit a cult" out of fear that he too will be "impressed" by what he sees and that he too may become an "apologist."

Lunde comments that for a scientist to be drawing conclusions about what he or she has never observed is absurd.[24] In all likelihood the response of Singer and others would be that they have conducted hundreds of interviews with *ex*-members, yet as will be explained fully in Chapter 5, to rely solely on former members of any group as one's source of scientific, objective data is dishonest and misleading.

Another scholar who has conducted extensive research on the Unification Church is religious studies professor Thomas McGowan. His 1979 study of 74 Unification Church members led him to conclude that "There is no evidence of so-called 'brainwashing' in either the written replies or the oral interviews." McGowan adds that most of those interviewed seemed to be relatively independent young men and women who in most cases had already rejected their childhood religion "long before accepting this new religion."[25]

The conclusion of experts Robbins and Anthony is that "the validity of brainwashing as a scientific concept is problematic, to say the least..." They write that brainwashing can be described as a mystifying and inherently subjective metaphor—which is now being used as a simplistic explanation for intense sectarian confinement, as well as a way of attacking groups against which charges of tangible physical coercion cannot be substantiated."[26] Gene James adds that "the primary function of the idea of brainwashing as applied to new religious groups has been to legitimate oppression."[27]

One important rationale for the brainwashing myth has been offered by researchers such as psychiatrist Lee Colemen. In his excellent expose, "Psychiatry The Faithbreaker," Colemen writes that brainwashing is simply an explanation for behavior with which people disagree. "The claim of 'brainwashing' today accomplishes what the claim of 'possession by the devil' accomplished hundreds of years ago....Today indeed critics can't accept the fact that many young people are finding fulfillment in some of these new churches, so they attribute their contentment to the effects of 'mind control.'[28] In a similar vein, Harvey Cox remarks:

> *Some psychiatrists contend that young people who join Oriental religious movements or Jesus communes have obviously been 'brainwashed' since they now share their money and have lost interest in becoming successful executives. That someone could freely choose a path of mystical devotion, self-sacrifice and the sharing of worldly goods seems self-evidently impossible to them. They forget that...according to the Gospel of Mark, Jesus was a candidate for 'deprogramming,' since his own family thought he was berserk and his religious leaders said he was possessed by the devil.*[29]

Researchers Alan Scheflin and Edward Opton in *The Mind Manipulators* suggest that "brainwashing" or "mind control" are convenient ways to rationalize one's actions and thereby avoid taking responsibility. Anyone can commit an act such as joining an unpopular group and afterwards claim "I was programmed to do so." Scheflin and Opton point out that esoteric notions such as "brainwashing" allow people to forget that they are responsible for their own actions. Personal values and independence of thought and judgment "are not snatched away from people....The concept of brainwashing is the most seductive mind manipulation of all."[30]

To charge that someone is "brainwashed" means that one can dismiss absolutely everything he has to say. It also means that one need not bother trying to find out what this person or group of persons actually believe. What makes the theory even more attractive is that one can dismiss anything that any sociologist, psychiatrist, theologian or clergyman says that is positive about this person or group of persons. Why? Because they must also be brainwashed! As absurd as this sounds, this kind of simplistic, yet bigoted attitude has been experienced by many Unification Church members.

Jeremiah S. Gutman, who is a leading figure in the American Civil Liberties Union and an active civil rights attorney, points out that through such a distorted and negative perspective "A religion becomes a cult; proselytization becomes brainwashing; persuasion becomes propaganda; missionaries become subversive agents; retreats, monasteries and convents become prisons; holy ritual becomes bizarre conduct; religious observance becomes aberrant behavior; devotion and meditation become psychopathic trances."[31]

Another sociologist who is well known for his extensive research on this subject, James T. Richardson of the University of Nevada, says that the so-called new religions or cults do not employ techniques of brainwashing. Speaking to a religious research conference co-sponsored by the University of Lethbridge, Alberta, he observed "I am unaware of anything like that going on in new religions." Instead he refers to the concept of brainwashing as another "boogyman" to explain people's involvement in new religious movements.[32] Trudy Solomon of the National Science Foundation concludes that "Labeling as brainwashing of any indoctrination, teaching, or philosophy that is engaged in voluntarily is surely an erroneous if not dangerous practice."[33]

Theologian Frank Flinn, in a recent article, "Criminalizing Conversion," cites Eileen Barker, *The Making of a Moonie* (1984), for the same point, Flinn asserts that through Barker's exhaustive five year investigation of the Unification Church, she has fully dispelled the myth that the Church "brainwashes" its members. "Her first hand statistics demonstrate that people who join are 'seekers' in the first place, that the retention rate is stunningly low, and that members can leave at any time with relative ease."[34]

Sociologists David Bromley and Anson Shupe state this same conclusion in unequivocal terms: "The entire concept of brainwashing, as we have seen, is a misnomer. It is repudiated by many sociologists, psychologists and psychiatrists as a crude euphemism. Worse, it is a distortion of a real, understandable process of attitude change that is neither mysterious nor unusual in American society."[35]

Impact of the Brainwashing Theory

Despite this overwhelming consensus, and the lack of any credible, empirical evidence to the contrary, there remains a small group of zealous advocates of the brainwashing theory. Unfortunately, by preying upon the fears of modern society, this group, generally known as the "anti-cult movement," has become successful in convincing much of society that such a thing as brainwashing (or variations on the same theme) is consistently practiced by new religious groups. So successful have they been that they are "distinguished" speakers at PTA meetings across America, and a major new textbook on psychiatry now contains an extremely distorted article on "cults." Religious studies professor William C. Shepherd summarizes this textbook article by saying that according to Louis West and Margaret Singer, cult membership by itself qualifies one for a psychiatric label and that conversion is "traumatic neurosis." Shepherd adds that John Clark refers to conversion as "temporal lobe epilepsy."[36]

Why has this group been so successful in shaping not only the opinions of our sociey but the organs of our educational institutions? The following chapters will highlight some of the key reasons.

References

1. Donald T. Lunde and Thomas E. Wilson, "Brainwashing as a Defense to Criminal Liability: Patty Hearst Revisited," *Criminal Law Bulletin,* vol. 13, 1977, 347-48. Psychiatrist Lee Coleman, in his article "Psychiatry the Faithbreaker" writes: "Out of this experience, however, and the embellishments of cold-war propaganda that sought to gain support for what was an unpopular war, came the idea that the Chinese had developed a method of 'mind control.'" The idea that scared so many people, as Coleman suggests, was "that a zombie could be created, one that acted like he was in control of his own thoughts and feelings but whose mind was in fact under someone else's control. It is this zombie that anti-cultists and vocal psychiatrists so vehemently claim the cults are fashioning." Lee Coleman, *Psychiatry the Faithbreaker: How psychiatry is promoting bigotry in America* (Sacramento: Printing Dynamics, 1982) 15. See also Joel Fort, "Mind Control: The What and How of Conversion and Indoctrination," supra, 220.

2. New York: Norton, 1961, 4.

3. Ibid.

4. Ibid., 420-37. For a detailed critique of each of Lifton's eight categories of Totalism, see Lee Coleman "New Religions and 'Deprogramming': Who's Brainwashing Whom?" in Thomas Robbins, William C. Shepherd and James McBride (eds.), *Cults, Culture and The Law* (Chico, CA: Scholars Press, 1985) 71.

5. In another major work on this topic, *Coercive Persuasion: A Socio-Psychological Analysis of the "Brainwashing" of American Civilian Prisoners by the Chinese Communists* (New York: North, 1961), Edgar Schein makes it clear that physical confinement or captivity is *essential* for "coercive persuasion" or "brainwashing." This has been strongly affirmed by Donald T. Lunde and Thomas E. Wilson, "Brainwashing as a Defense to Criminal Liability: Patty Hearst Revisited," *Criminal Law Bulletin,* Vol. 13, 1977, 351.

6. Lifton, supra, 454-61. Sociologists David Bromley and Anson Shupe throw cold water on Lifton's theory. Following a lengthy analysis of his theory they conclude as follows: "the psychiatric literature on brainwashing, which anti-cultists frequently cite but which they apparently have never read carefully, makes no sweeping claims about terrifyingly effective methods of subverting human reason....While much has been made of so-called brainwashing or thought-reform techniques as some little-known set of powerful procedures that devious communists discovered, these techniques actually represent fairly straightforward extensions of basic principles in psychological conditioning and group dynamics. These same principles are routinely applied in psychiatric therapy, in learning situations by weight control groups, in alcohol and drug abuse correction, by industrial psychologists, and even in mass media advertising. Under certain conditions they can be relatively effective, but they are far from foolproof. What really struck postwar observers of abused POW's as shocking, therefore, was not the existence of such attitude-change techniques per se but their use in psychological warfare. This is an important point to remember when anticultists claim that cults employ sinister, as yet poorly understood mind-control techniques: *Such techniques even where it can be shown they are used, are neither mysterious nor new, nor have they nearly the effectiveness attributed to them by popular writers."* (emphasis in original) David Bromley & Anson Shupe, *Strange Gods* (Boston: Beacon Press, 1981) 99-100.

7. See Thomas Robbins, Wm. C. Shepherd and James McBride (eds.), *Cults, Culture and The Law* (Chico, CA: Scholars Press, 1985) 59.

8. Robert N. Shapiro, "Indoctrination, Personhood, and Religious Beliefs," in Thomas Robbins, William C. Shepherd and James McBride (eds.), *Cults, Culture, and the Law* (Chico, CA: Scholars Press, 1985) 153.

9. Herbert Richardson (ed.), *New Religions and Mental Health* (New York: Edwin Mellen, 1980) xiii. Lowell Streiker cites Lieutenant Colonel Ralph C. Wood, USMC retired, who during his twenty-two years of active duty closely examined the "brainwashing" techniques practiced by the Chinese, North Koreans, and North Vietnamese. Streiker quoted Wood's response to Dr. Clark's 1977 testimony before the Vermont legislature: "Dr. Clark strongly implies that 'cult' religions use brainwashing techniques to convert and hold their followers when actually the techniques he describes are NOT brainwashing and to label them as such is a dangerous encroachment on basic liberties." Lowell Streiker, *Mind-Bending,* (New York: Doubleday, 1984) 162.

10. Thomas Szasz, "Some Call It Brainwashing," *The New Republic,* March 6, 1976. *See also* Note, "Conservatorships and Religious Cults: Divining A Theory of Free Exercise," *New York University Law Journal,* Vol. 53, 1978, 1282.

11. Streiker, supra, 153.

12. Ibid., 154.

13. Ibid.

14. "Interview with Harvey Cox" in Steven J. Gelberg (ed.), *Hare Krishna, Hare Krishna* (New York: Grove Press, 1983) 50.

15. Walter Reich, "Brainwashing, Psychiatry, and the Law," *Psychiatry* Vol. 39, Nov. 1976, 402.

16. Dick Anthony & Thomas Robbins, "New Religions, Families and 'Brainwashing'," in Thomas Robbins & Dick Anthony (eds.), *In Gods We Trust* (New Brunswick, NJ: Transaction, 1981) 264-65. See also Robbins and Anthony," Available Research is...not consistent with a model of psychological kidnapping," in Joseph Rubinstein and Brent D. Slife (eds.), *Taking Sides: Clashing Views on Controversial Psychological Issues,* 2d ed., (Guilford, CT: Dushkin, 1982) 329.

17. Donald T. Lunde & Henry A. Sigal, "Use and Abuse of DSM-III in 'Cult' Litigation." (not yet published, retained in author's files).

18. Gene G. James, "Brainwashing: The Myth and The Actuality," *Thought, Fordham University Quarterly*, Vol. LXI, June, 1986, 249.

19. Ibid., 254.

20. Eileen Barker, *The Making of Moonie* (Oxford: Basil Blackwell, 1984) 134.

21. See for example, Gregory Tillett, "The Moonies, The Media and Religious Persecution" (unpublished, author's files) 1982.

22. Donald T. Lunde, interview with author, Aug. 3, 1986

23 Louis Jolyn West, "Contemporary Cults—Utopian Image, Internal Reality," *The Center Magazine*, March/April 1982, 11. John Clark also admits that he has never attended Unification Church programs. See, for example *Keiffer v. Holy Spirit Association*, U.S. District Court, Dist. of New Hampshire, Civil No. 77-381D, Testimony of John G. Clark, July 23, 1980, 116.

24. Interview with author Aug. 3, 1986.

25. Thomas McGowan, "Conversion: A Theological View" in Herbert Richardson (ed.), *New Religions and Mental Health* (New York: Edwin Mellen, 1980) 167.

26. T. Robbins and D. Anthony, "Brainwashing and the Persecution of Cults," *Journal of Religion and Health*, Vol. 19, No. 1, 1980, 66.

27. James, supra, 255.

28. L. Coleman, *Psychiatry The Faithbreaker*, supra, 16.

29. *The New York Times*, Feb. 16, 1977, 25, col. 1, cited in Laurence H. Tribe, *American Constitutional Law* (Mineola, NY: Foundation Press, 1978) 884.

30. Alan W. Scheflin & Edward M. Opton, Jr., *The Mind Manipulators* (New York: Paddington Press, 1978) 474.

31. Jeremiah S. Gutman, quoted in Robert Shapiro, "Indoctrination, Personhood and Religious Beliefs," supra, 153.

32. "Brainwashing not used by new religious cults," *The Lethbridge Herald* (Lethbridge, Alberta, Canada), March 12, 1983. A 1980 article carried a similiar headline about Prof. Richardson: "Sociologist: New religious groups don't brainwash young converts," *The Gazette-Journal* (Reno, Nevada) June 19, 1980.

33. Trudy Solomon, "Programming and Deprogramming, the Moonies: Social Psychology Applied," in D. Bromley & J. Richardson (eds.), *The Brainwashing/Deprogramming Controversy* (New York: Edwin Mellen, 1983) 179.

34. Frank K. Flinn, "Criminalizing Conversion: The Legislative Assault on New Religions *et al*," 17, forthcoming in James Day & William Laufer (eds.), *Crimes, Values and Religion* (Norwood, NJ: Ablex Publishing, 1986). See also Eileen Barker, *The Making of a Moonie* (New York: Blackwell, 1984).

35. Bromley & Shupe, *Strange Gods*, supra, 124.

36. See William C. Shepherd, *To Secure the Blessings of Liberty* (New York: Crossroad Publishing, 1985), 115. Another major textbook by Sueann Ambron & Neil Salkind, *Child Development*, 4th ed. (New York: Holt, Rinehart and Winston, 1984) also contains an extremely biased and hostile description of the "Cults" at page 499. As a source of additional information, it suggests only organizations which are committed to the destruction of new religions such as the American Family Foundation (AFF), the leading anti-cult organization in the United States. When confronted with this bias, a representative of the publisher admitted: 'It sounds like a cheap shot; very unscholarly.' Author's telephone interview, July 16, 1986.

Chapter 3

THE MENTAL HEALTH PROFESSION

Religion as Mental Illness

Sigmund Freud, the founder of modern psychiatry, asserted that religion was a form of mental illness. Of course he was not the first to take such a position. Herbert Richardson suggests that Freud was following in "the continuing anti-religious tradition since Voltaire—or Rabelais or Lucretius." Richardson says such individuals have "repeatedly claimed that religious adherence is an irrational and unfree act of persons who are manipulated by priests who prey on their guilt and fear."[1]

Freud traced much of the neurosis of individuals to repressed sexuality, and this helped lead him to his anti-religious views since religion was seen as repressing sexual desires. The view of Freud and others was that religious doctrine is invariably employed in a manipulative manner to subvert reason, which makes it "deceptively exploitive of certain universal human needs."[2]

The noted Swiss-born author and Catholic priest, Hans Kung, addressed this point in a widely publicized speech to the 1986 convention of the American Psychiatric Association. He asserted that academic psychiatry treats religion not as "a positive force toward health or healing" but "usually in a negative form."

Father Kung said that for most psychiatrists religion "hardly plays a constructive role" in their professional life, their research or their therapeutic practice. He added, "some psychiatrists are decidedly anti-religious: Religion is neurosis or psychosis, at all events an illness requiring a cure." [3]

In a recent paper by sociologists Brock Kilbourne and James T. Richardson, entitled "Anti-Religious Bias in the Diagnostic and Statistical Manual (DSM) III: The Case of the Cults," the authors express grave concern about recent developments in modern psychiatry which are leading to a more negative view of religion. They point to the growing acceptance of psychiatric definitions of mental disorder which are used to "psychiatrize" or "medicalize" membership in new religions despite "their empirically weak and inconsistent data base." [4]

Aside from Lifton's book on "Totalism," one of the most well-known "bibles" of the anti-cult movement is a book called *Snapping* by Flo Conway and Jim Siegelman.[5] Gordon Melton of the religious studies department of the University of California, Santa Barbara and director of the Institute for the Study of American Religion, along with Robert Moore of the Chicago Theological Seminary, write that this book "reflects a militantly secularist reductionistic and regressive reading of religious experience characteristic of classic Freudian and other hostile interpretations of religion in general and conversion in particular."[6]

Lifton, Clark and Singer

This is precisely the attitude of the handful of proponents of the "brainwashing," "mind control," "thought control," "coercive persuasion" thesis. Robert Lifton, for instance, writes about "destructive cults" with their "totalistic" environments, where adherents are subjected to what he calls "thought reform." According to Lifton, they are also subjected to profound threats to their personal autonomy and are deprived of a combination of external information and inner reflection.[7] Worst of all, Lifton asserts, "thought reform" makes a "demand for purity." This phenomenon is such that "the experiential world is sharply divided into the pure and the impure, the absolutely good and the absolutely evil...Nothing human is immune from the stern moral judgments. All 'taints' and 'poisons' which contribute to the existing state of impurity must be searched out and eliminated."[8]

Lifton argues that this is destructive because, in actual practice, no one can ever achieve the level of perfection demanded. Therefore, the demand for purity becomes a means to instill a powerful sense of guilt and shame which demands "that one strive permanently and painfully for something which not only does not exist but is in fact alien to the human condition."[9]

By applying such an attack against the new religions, Lifton is actually attacking all religious ideals. He is also attacking concepts that are inherent in nearly all religions. This is particularly evident in Lifton's attack upon the concept of "guilt." While he acknowledges that "guilt and shame are basic to human existence," he makes guilt seem like a concept that religion ought not tamper with.[10] This fits in perfectly with the beliefs of those who have applied Lifton's analysis, since they apparently do not accept religious values as being valid.

John Clark has adopted Lifton's thesis and taken it to a further extreme. He is so convinced that some religious groups are "destructive cults" that he has signed sworn statements that adherents were mentally incompetent without ever having met them or examined them. In the case of Hare Krishna member Ed Shapiro, Clark testified in court that Mr. Shapiro was "incompetent as a result of mind control" despite having never even met or examined him![11]

Based on Clark's testimony, Shapiro was forced to enter a mental hospital. After two weeks, the psychiatrists at the prestigious McLean Psychiatric Hospital decided that they disagreed with Clark's order, finding no evidence of *any* mental disorder.[12] Despite this finding, Clark argued that they had just not looked hard enough, because when someone is under "mind control" normal evaluation methods do not work. It was necessary, he claimed, to remove Shapiro from his religious environment. Clark alleged that Shapiro was one of those "people who have trouble facing reality of their own inner selves" and, as a result, chose membership in an "absolutist cult" as a mode of controlling his feelings and actions.[13]

In writing on this subject, Berkeley psychiatrist Lee Coleman suggests that Clark was really saying that "the act of joining an unpopular religion was *in itself a sign of mental illness.*"[14] Lowell Streiker, who is the founder and executive director of the well-known Freedom Counseling Center and who himself tends to take a rather critical view of the new religions, has harsh words for Clark's analysis. After a lengthy description of Clark's opinion that members of "religious cults" suffer from an ailment which he terms "prolonged dissociation," Streiker points out that:

> *prolonged dissociative states are extremely common in our society. They are found everywhere—alcoholism, drug abuse, television addiction, jogging, immersion in rock music played on a Walkman, gambling, sex,*

> *Jazzercise, speaking in tongues, knitting, singing in the church choir, sponsoring a Little League baseball team, selling Amway products, practicing yoga, et cetera, et cetera ad nauseam.*

Streiker adds that almost any form of enthusiasm or any lack of enthusiasm could be "trance-inducing." He writes:

> *Habitual unconsciousness may be harmful to one's well-being. But cults scarcely have the monopoly on habitual unconsiousness which Clark suggests. Further, I am amazed to note that Clark developed his theory on the basis of a small statistical sample. He states in his article, 'The Manipulation of Madness,' in which his theory is fully elaborated, that he had examined '50 individuals' in a four-year span. In addition, I note that although Clark credits cults with all sorts of devastation to the central nervous system, he has not hospitalized a patient in years.*[15]

The Shapiro case eventually led to an investigation and a severe reprimand against Clark by the Massachusetts Board of Registration and Discipline in Medicine. The Massachusetts Board stated that "There is no recognized diagnostic category of mental illness of 'thought reform and mind control.'" The Board added: "Moreover, the basis on which this 'diagnosis' was made seems inadequate, as mere membership in a religious organization can never, standing alone, be a sufficient basis for diagnosis of mental illness...."[16]

Unfortunately, this did little to stop Clark's unconventional and appalling practice. He continued to follow this procedure for some time. In a number of similar instances, he gave sworn testimony that members of the Unification Church were subject to "mind control" simply by virtue of the fact of their membership in the church. One of those people subsequently filed a complaint to this same Massachusetts Board of Registration and Discipline in Medicine. In an affidavit, this woman stated that without knowing her or speaking to her, Clark "had testified in a civil trial that he believed that I was under mind control and suffered from various other mental disorders."[17]

In addition, a number of his fellow anti-cultists have engaged in similar practices. One incident was the case of *David Molko and Tracy Leal v. Unification Church (HSA).* This involved two former Unification Church members who had been forcibly "deprogrammed" and who eventually filed a lawsuit against the church. (For a more detailed explanation of this case, see Chapter 8). Neither Molko nor Leal was examined during their membership in the church. Nevertheless, many months later, psychologist Margaret Singer and psychiatrist Samuel Benson had no problem giving sworn testimony that both Molko and Leal had been under "coercive persuasion" during their membership in the Unification Church. This presumption was not lost on Judge Stuart Pollak, who commented as follows in his order granting summary judgment in favor of the defendant Unification Church:

> *Both doctors examined the Plaintiffs long after the events in question. They did not reach their opinions concerning Plaintiffs' state of mind based upon a contemporaneous examination independent of their views of Unification Church methods, but seem to have reasoned backwards from their disapproval of those methods to the conclusion that Plaintiffs were not thinking freely because they were persuaded by them.*[18]

Margaret Singer, along with John Clark, continues to be one of the most outspoken advocates of "brainwashing" and related terms of disapproval of the so-called "cults." Yet as the above-cited example demonstrates, her "research" is highly conclusory and unscientific. Brock Kilbourne and James T. Richardson note that Singer along with John Clark, Flo Conway and Jim Siegelman have come up with reports of negative effects of membership in new religions that have several disconcerting methodological problems. Their reports show an "overreliance on nonstatistical and qualitative data, biased samples, a failure to consider alternative explanations, retrospective self-reports and...a failure to apply proper statistical techniques to quantitative data."[19]

Kilbourne and Richardson point out that some psychiatric terminology such as DSM-III (derived from *The Diagnostic and Statistical Manual of Mental Disorders* 3rd ed.) has been improperly used to label members of new religions. They write that DSM-III is "conspicuously vague." Nevertheless, "it is being used as a 'catch-all' for labeling anything that might resemble, no matter how remote or unsubstantiated, some kind of a dissociative reaction...Somehow the vagueness and absence of sound empirical data supporting this diagnosis have continued to go unnoticed."[20]

During a recent trial, *Wollersheim v. Church of Scientology,* Singer testified that there are six "parameters" involved in "thought reform" as practiced by "the cults." They include a program of control over one's time, inducing powerlessness, inhibiting old behavior, eliciting new behavior, keeping the person uninformed that this process is taking place, and finally, making him a part of a totalitarian organization.

Psychiatrist Thomas Szasz, who notes that Singer is not certified as a clinical psychologist by the American Psychological Association,[21] refutes her testimony in rather unequivocal terms. He says he does not believe that the term "thought reform" used by Singer and others can be considered an objective term. He questions whether there is a distinction between "thought reform" and any other manner of influencing people's opinions and behaviors. Szasz states that it is rather common to all religions, thought systems, schools and military associations to influence or "reform" people's thoughts. He says people go to these institutions in order to submit to them and learn something, to change their opinions and way of life. He adds that to call "something thought reform pretentiously prejudges it and makes it look like a scientific judgment, whereas, in fact, it only implies that the observer does not like that particular enterprise."[22]

A further example of Singer's unorthodox methodology was seen in her testimony in another case involving a former member of the church of Scientology. Her total sample for the sweeping generalizations she made about this church were five Scientologists, four of whom had already left the group. As one writer exclaims, "It is difficult to imagine any anthropologist willing to generalize on some exotic community on such a slender basis."[23]

Despite this slender empirical data-base, Singer boldly asserted that her "evidence" showed that former members were widely marked by their habit of staring, by increased weight, pallor, poor dental hygiene, stringy, oily hair, and general physical deterioration. Further, she provided no statistical data to substantiate these assertions, which led Louis H. Gann, a senior Fellow at Stanford's Hoover Institution, to conclude about Singer's "studies:"

> *Her work, unfortunately, suffers from a variety of disabilities. These include a lack of historical perspective; an inadequate knowledge of comparative theology necessary for a researcher concerned with the subject of religion; an apparent failure to grasp the varieties of religious motivation; a seeming unwillingness to consider adherence to unorthodox—or even bizarre—religions as a legitimate form of behavior guaranteed under the constitution; and a remarkable propensity for drawing sweeping conclusions from inadequate evidence.*[24]

In light of Singer's methodology, one might speculate as to how the American public might react if a report on the Roman Catholic Church was done solely on the basis of interviews with a small number of apostate priests and nuns. It is unlikely that this would be accepted as objective or fair. Nevertheless, as Franklin Littell of Temple University points out, Margaret Singer and a small coterie of these people travel the nation and the world, like "ambulance-chasers," testifying at trials and investigative hearings about various new religious movements they do not like, all the while receiving very substantial fees.[25]

Beneficial Effects of New Religions

Contrary to the opinion of Singer and her followers, sociologists have reported numerous beneficial or therapeutic effects of membership in groups such as the Unification Church. Thomas Robbins and Dick Anthony point to frequent termination of drug use, decrease in neurotic distress, decrease in suicidal tendencies, renewed vocational motivation and self-actualization, decrease in moral confusion and psychosomatic symptoms, increase in social compassion and responsibility, clarification of ego identity and general positive therapeutic and problem-solving assistance.[26]

Despite the anti-religious bias in the profession, three psychological studies have confirmed this view. In an extensive study of Unification Church members, psychiatrist Marc Galanter told the American Psychiatric Association that "conversion apparently provided considerable and sustained relief from neurotic distress."[27] Another psychiatrist, J. Thomas Ungerleider concludes from his study: "A person who joined a religious movement, made its work his life, and eventually rose through its hierarchy to an elite position probably gained a better experience than those who never experience this phenomenon at all."[28]

A Canadian study by psychiatrists Saul Levine and N.E. Salter also gives grudging tribute to the new religions. In a report entitled "Youth and contemporary religious movements: psychosocial findings," they state: "These religions, as fatuous and as reprehensible as most people may find them, are improving the personal lives of many of their members."[29]

Levine, who worked in conjunction with a Government of Ontario Study, reports that members of new religious groups, like members of traditional religious groups, appear generally normal. In his view, there are some who have symptoms of psychological illness, but his studies indicate that this condition frequently antedated membership in the religious group.[30]

The real problem, as uncovered by Levine's research, is not that new religious groups act in unhealthy ways. Rather, the problem lies with psychiatrists or psychologists such as Lifton, Clark and Singer, who assert that members of various new religions—who exhibit no empirical symptoms of any mental dysfunction—are under mental coercion and are not voluntarily doing what they freely chose to do. Their view is that these believers did not know they were acting involuntarily—despite the fact that there was no behavioral abnormality to corroborate that claim. In short, the Clark and Singer school of thought is that the "only symptom of their sickness was that they belonged to a religious group with which the psychiatrist disagreed!"[31]

This is reminiscent of many other flagrant experiences of psychiatric bigotry in our history. For example, 19th century slave owners from the South coined a psychological illness "drapetomania," or "the insane desire to wander away from home," to explain and discredit this "tendency" of black slaves to run away. The term "drapeto," which is now listed in medical dictionaries, was coined, and the "disease-state" to which it refers was "discovered" (or invented) in 1850. In that year, the Louisiana State Medical Society appointed a commission of its members, headed by the distinguished physician Samuel Cartwright, to look into and to report back on the physical and psychical peculiarities of the Negro race. One of the psychological "peculiarities" of the Negro race reported by the commission was that this race included individuals who tended to run away.[32] This example shows how a person who engages in behavior that is not in conformity with the established order can easily be defined as "not healthy."

Much of the argument advanced by Clark, Singer and others is not new. What is new, Herbert Richardson suggests, "is the creation of the brainwashing concept' *as the name of a disease and the existence of a group of medical professionals* who seek to be empowered to treat it."[33]

Competition to Displace Religion

Some scholars assert that the basis for the tremendous animosity between some members of the mental health profession and new religious groups is nothing more than competition, since both claim to provide effective knowledge about the life of the soul. Herbert Richardson asks: "How then, can it be presumed that psychiatrists do not have a stake in excluding religious leaders from 'the care of souls' in order to increase their own share of the business?"[34]

A similar view is set forth by Thomas Robbins and Dick Anthony in their study "Cults Versus Shrinks: Psychiatry and the Control of Religious Movements:"

1. *"Cults" and "shrinks" are competitors,* i.e., many persons attempt to improve themselves or resolve their difficulties with the assistance of Scientology or gurus instead of employing "legitimate" therapists;

2. Religious "deprogramming" and auxiliary service for the "rehabilitation of cultists and ex-cultists expand vocational opportunities for psychiatrists and psychologists as well as for social workers, lawyers, detectives, clergy, and ex-devotees.[35]

Sociologists Brock Kilbourne and James T. Richardson make a similar assertion in their 1984 article "Psychotherapy and New Religions in a Pluralistic Society." They suggest that psychologists and psychiatrists have seized the role once bestowed upon the clergy as today's "new seers" with a "hidden truth." In effect, the mental health profession and religions are "competing for clients, conceptual territory—that is, who will define reality, fantasy, health, mental illness, self, and so forth."[36]

In another paper entitled, "Anti-Religion Bias in the Diagnostic and Statistical Manual [DSM] III: The Case of the Cults," Kilbourne and Richardson point to "unsubstantiated claims of psychopathology in cult members" and the tendency among many psychiatrists and psychologists to presume that a member of a new religion "is sick or guilty by association." They report that these mental health professionals generally believe that membership in these religious groups is harmful and that the only "cure" is removal. Kilbourne and Richardson express concern about the "untempered intervention" and increasing role of psychiatry and psychology in contemporary American society. They refer to them as today's "secular priests," labeling their "reckless use of power and abuse of power" as "sinister."[37]

In a subsequent article, Kilbourne and Richardson assert that members of the mental health profession have acted as "social control agents" to frighten young people away from the new groups. They express concern about the growing efforts of some members of the mental health profession to "medicalize"[38] and "psychiatrize"[39] involvement in new religions.[40]

Attack on Religion

Although it is often not overt, this anti-religious bias can be discerned in the testimony, the writings and the activities of the anti-cult movement. They profess to be attacking only a select group of intense believers or what they call "destructive cults." However, when one looks closely at the beliefs and practices of the groups they are attacking, their anti-religious intentions and motivation become apparent. One example is the frequent criticism that the "cults" make people feel loved, cared for and secure; that they provide answers to the questions of life and a sense of meaning and purpose. Margaret Singer acknowledges that, in many instances, "the cult" promised—and for many provided—a solution to their feelings of distress. As Singer herself writes, "Cults supply ready-made friendships and ready-made decisions about careers, dating, sex, and marriage, and they outline a clear 'meaning of life'."[41] Singer also points out that their experience taught some adherents to overcome their fear of rejection and to "connect more openly and warmly to other people."[42]

Nevertheless, according to detractors such as Singer, it is an insidious thing that people find happiness in groups that do not conform to the status quo or the mainstream of society. But the real questions has to be, Who defines happiness? Does society have a right to impose its concept of success and happiness on individuals? If members of a Catholic nunnery or the U.S. Marines or the San Francisco 49ers or the Unification Church think they are happy, who has a right to tell them otherwise?

The alarming aspect of all this is that, even though atheists have expressed anti-religious sentiments for many years, it is only recently that religion has been so seriously attacked. Many religious leaders have expressed alarm that American society has become increasingly secularized in recent years. To a substantial degree, religion has been placed on the defensive.

It is interesting to note that the religions that have been targetted as "destructive cults" are nearly always small religious groups with a strong evangelical fervor. The Clarks, the Singers and other anti-cultists know that they would lose credibility if they attacked religion on a wholesale basis. Therefore, it is safer and more acceptable to attack the smaller minority groups—and the easiest way is to label them with pseudo-medical terminology, prescribing psychological therapy.[43] As psychiatrist Peter Breggin points out, this form of attack was used by the Nazis in Germany[44] and as theologian Richard Rubenstein and others assert, this is a method employed by the Soviet Union to oppress its dissidents today.[45]

> Lee Coleman describes it this way:
> *"Because the religions under attack are generally unpopular, it has been easy for many to overlook the fact that such tactics once unleashed on some may eventually be unleashed on us all. Under the cover of psychiatric expertise and benevolence, indeed, there is no one who would escape the possibility of mental evaluation—evaluation to determine if his choice were made with a free mind or manipulated one."*[46]

This is not to say that new religious movements, like other structured religious disciplines, do not exert a powerful influence over their members' lifestyles and beliefs. Coleman warns that "If the Unification Church, Scientology and Hare Krishnas are engaging in brainwashing and mind control, then so are the "Big Three" (Catholics, Protestants and Jews), not to mention the Boy Scouts, Little League and Madison Avenue. Shall we send all their 'victims' to psychiatrists?"[47]

As pointed out in this chapter, not all members of the mental health profession are responsible for the attacks on new religions. Nevertheless, these attacks pose a serious problem, a problem that threatens the free exercise of all religions.

References

1. See Herbert Richardson (ed.), *New Religions and Mental Health* (New York: Edwin Mellen, 1980) xv. In all fairness to the mental health profession, their anti-religious bias can be seen as part of a larger process of secularization which has affected all of society.

2. *Molko and Leal v. HSA,* 179 Cal. App. 3d 450, 471 (1986). See also James Strachey (ed.), *Sigmund Freud, The Future of an Illusion* (Garden City, N.Y.: Doubleday, 1964); and testimony of Dr. Thomas Szasz in *Wollersheim v. Church of Scientology,* Superior Court of California, Los Angeles County, No. C 332027, June 18, 1986, 12, 212.

3. Hans Kung, "Religion: The Final Taboo?", *Origins,* May 29, 1986, 27.

4. Brock K. Kilbourne and James T. Richardson, "Anti-Religious Bias in the Diagnostic and Statistical Manual [DSM] III: The Case of the Cults," presented to the Annual Meeting for the Scientific Study of Religion, Chicago, 1984, 1-2.

5. Flo Conway & Jim Siegelman, *Snapping: America's Epidemic of Sudden Personality Change* (New York: Delta, 1979).

6. J. Gordon Melton & Robert L. Moore, *The Cult Experience* (New York: Pilgrim Press, 1982) 41.

7. Lifton, supra, 419-21. Although Lifton's theory has been distorted by members of the anti-cult movement beyond his original intention, it is useful to describe some of his views since they have been so widely reported.

8. Ibid., 423.

9. Ibid., 423-424.

10. Ibid., 424.

11. Affidavit of Sept. 29, 1976, submitted to the Supreme Court of New York in *People v. Murphy* #2012-76. See also Coleman, supra, 7.

12. Coleman, supra, 8.

13. Ibid.

14. Ibid. See also Streiker, supra, 159.

15. Streiker, supra, 161.

16. Ibid., 157. Streiker quotes further from the report: "There seems no factual basis," the Board concluded, "either for the conclusion that Mr. Shapiro was mentally ill or that he was a danger to himself. Again, this invites the concern that the judgments were based entirely on the subject's religion." Ibid. See also Coleman, supra, 18.

17. Affidavit of Jana Keiffer, dated September 22, 1981, author's files. See also Testimony of John Clark in *Keiffer v. Holy Spirit Association,* supra, where Clark admits that his diagnosis of Jana Keiffer as being under "mind control" involved some "guesswork." Ibid., 86. Lowell Streiker gives further examples of this same practice by Clark in cases involving members of the Church of Scientology and those who had gone through est training. Streiker, supra, 157-58.

18. *Molko and Leal v. HSA,* supra, 16, n.9.

19. Brock K. Kilbourne and James T. Richardson, "Psychotherapy and New Religions in a Pluralistic Society," *American Psychological Association,* Vol. 39, No. 3, 1984, 9-10, fn. 1.

20. Brock K. Kilbourne and James T. Richardson, "Cultphobia," *Thought, Fordham University Quarterly,* Vol. LXI, June 1986, 264.

21. *Wollersheim,* supra, 12,164.

22. Ibid., 12,166-67. Szasz, who is in at least seven Who's Who listings including "Who's Who in Medicine," added that Singer's use of the word "parameters" is faulty. He stated that "parameters is a pretentious, scientific sounding word. There are no parameters here. She has made up six categories. This is not written in stone." He added that there "is a saying about this kind of thing in scientific literature and research. It is called accurate reporting of inaccurate data." Ibid., 12,176. Szasz later stated that Singer's description of Wollersheim's "thought reform program" had no "scientific validity at all. Again, it is an illustration of advocacy disguised as science or pseudo-science."Ibid., 12,188.

23. See Louis H. Gann, "Dr. Margaret Singer: An Evaluation of Her Work," Hoover Institution, Stanford University, (unpublished, retained in author's files) 8.

24. Ibid., 1.

25. Franklin H. Littell, "American Rules About 'Sects' and 'Cults'" *Proclaim Liberty!*, FHL: 116, 2. (Author's files)

26. See Thomas Robbins and Dick Anthony, "Deprogramming, brainwashing and the medicalization of deviant religious groups," *Social Problems,* Vol. 29, 1982, 283-297. This view finds support in Brock K. Kilbourne and James T. Richardson, "Psychotherapy and New Religions in a Pluralistic Society," *American Psychological Association,* Vol. 39, No. 3, 1984, 6.

27. Marc Galanter, "The 'Moonies,' a psychological study," Presented to 131st Annual Meeting of the American Psychiatric Assn., Atlanta, GA, 1978, 10.

28. J. Thomas Ungerleider, *The New Religions* (New York: Merck, Sharp and Dohme, 1979) 15-16.

29. Saul V. Levine and N.E. Salter, "Youth and contemporary religious movements: psychosocial findings," *Canadian Psychiatric Assoc. Journal,* Vol. 21, 1976, 418.

30. Saul Levine, "Report on Physical and Mental Health Aspects of Religious Cults and Mind Bending Groups," cited in Daniel Hill, *Study of Mind Development Groups, Sects and Cults in Ontario: A Report to the Ontario Government* (Toronto: The Queen's Printer, 1980) 703.

31. Ibid. See also Herbert Richardson, supra, xiv.

32. Dr. Stephen Chorover, Professor of Brain Science at Massachusetts Institute of Technology, elaborated on this repulsive example of the abuse of psychiatry in his article "Mental Health as a Social Weapon" in Herbert Richardson (ed.), *New Religions and Mental Health,* supra, 16-17.

33. Herbert Richardson, supra, xv.

34. Ibid., xxv.

35. Ibid.

36. Brock K. Kilbourne and James T. Richardson, "Psychotherapy and New Religions," supra, 2, 11.

37. Brock K. Kilbourne and James T. Richardson, "Anti-Religion Bias in the Diagnostic and Statistical Manual [DSM] III: The Case of the Cults," presented to the Annual meeting of the Society for the Scientific Study of Religion, Chicago, Illinois, 1984, 36-38.

38. Thomas Robbins and Dick Anthony, "Deprogramming, brainwashing and the medicalization of deviant religious groups," *Social Problems,* Vol. 29, 1982, 283-297.

39. D. Kecmanovic "Psychiatrization: A General View," *The International Journal of Social Psychiatry,* Vol. 29, 1983, 308-31.

40. Brock K. Kilbourne and James T. Richardson, "Social Experimentation Self-Process or Social Role," *The International Journal of Social Psychiatry,* Vol. 31, 1985, 19.

41. Margaret Singer, "Coming Out of the Cults,"*Psychology Today,* Jan., 1976, 72.

42. Ibid., 80.

43. See, for example, William S. Bainbridge, "Religious Insanity in America: The Official Nineteenth-Century Theory," *Sociological Analysis,* Vol. 45, 1984, 237.

44. See Peter R. Breggin, "The Psychiatric Holocaust," *Penthouse,* 81 (retained in author's files).

45. See Richard Rubenstein,"Who Shall Define Reality For Us?", in Herbert Richardson (ed.), *New Religions and Mental Health,* supra, 9. See also Chorover, supra, 19; "Inside a Mind Jail: A Soviet Dissident gets the treatment at a mental hospital in Moscow," *Newsweek,* Aug. 11, 1986, 26.

46. Coleman, supra, 35-36.

47. Ibid., 17.

Chapter 4

DEPROGRAMMING/FAITHBREAKING

In recent years, the practice of "deprogramming" or "faithbreaking" has become less common.[1] In fact, to the general public, it has almost been unheard of over the past few years. The attacks on the Unification Church by the anti-cult people have become more "sophisticated," focusing more attention on "legal" attacks such as the tax prosecution of Rev. Moon and other legal challenges, as will be explained in Chapter 8. Nevertheless, it is important to understand the deprogramming controversy since it has been one of the major sources and expressions of fear and hostility toward new religions.

The Nature of Deprogramming

The alleged mental illness called "brainwashing" or "mind control" is presumably so severe and damaging that drastic measures must be taken. According to Clark, Singer and others, adherents of certain religious "cults" must be forcibly removed and subjected to "coercive deprogramming" or "faithbreaking," or otherwise they will never be able to leave the "cult." They take this view despite the following points:

1. They admit that traditional and "acceptable" religions and psychotherapists engage in practices similar to the "cults;"

2. They are unable to find any significant *clinical* evidence that the adherents were damaged by the new religions;

3. The "children" in question are over-age-of-majority adults;

4. It has been widely shown that members are able to leave, have left freely, and that 9 out of 10 who attend seminars or retreats never join.[2]

The term "deprogramming" has been used to describe a rather bizarre phenomenon that became prevalent during the 1970s involving the kidnapping of young adults by their own parents. To many people in contemporary society the incarceration of a human being for holding certain beliefs that may be contrary to "conventional" beliefs seems incredible. Nevertheless, it has happened with alarming frequency within a certain sector of the population.

The basic thrust of a "deprogramming" is essentially a "faithbreaking," or a breaking down of one's trust and belief in something. Thus, deprogramming is better referred to as faithbreaking because it is actually a ripping out or stripping of one's most cherished beliefs and ideals. It involves abducting members of religious (or other) groups, confining them and subjecting them to prolonged emotional and psychological pressure until they renounce the religious affiliation and beliefs of which the "deprogrammer" disapproves.[3]

This pseudo-therapy has been applied to the members of a wide range of religious groups from Roman Catholics, Episcopalians,[4] Seventh Day Adventists, Pentecostal Christians[5] and fundamentalist Christian groups[6], to the Unification Church, Jews for Jesus, The Way International and the Hare Krishna movement. Even more remarkably, deprogramming has been imposed on individuals belonging to political or special interest groups such as the Socialist Labor Party, lesbians[7] and to persons not belonging to any particular group at all, as in the case of two Denver women who were abducted by deprogrammers to be brought back into the strict tutelage of their Greek Orthodox parents.[8]

Perhaps the case that shocked the public most was the abduction and imprisonment for 31 days of San Francisco Bay area English professor Susan Wirth by deprogrammer Ted Patrick. Ms. Wirth said she was handcuffed to a bed, deprived of food and sleep and subjected to a battery of mind games designed to break her will. The reason was that Ms. Wirth's parents thought their daughter, at age 35, had become "too liberal" in her views because of her involvement with left wing pro-abortion, anti-racist and anti-death-penalty organizations. Her mother was reported to have paid $27,000 for the attempted deprogramming,[9] although San Francisco police officials suspect that the amount was as high as $40,000.[10]

The deprogramming or faithbreaking process begins with physically isolating and incarcerating the victim. This is often done by abduction, although it sometimes occurs when the adherent is visiting family or friends, at which time deprogrammers are brought in. In the case of abduction, a common method used to gain physical control involves waiting for the victim to appear alone on a street or other public place. The victim can then be physically forced into a car and taken to a site chosen by the deprogrammers.[11] Next the victim is taken to a place where he is cut off from everyone but his captors.[12] The site is often secured against anticipated escape attempts by using a second floor room in a motel with a separate entrance, with windows nailed shut, all doors locked and all telephones removed.

In later years, it became popular to use an isolated house, far from any possible observation.[13] Usually the deprogrammer is assisted by ex-members of the same religious group who were previously deprogrammed and "other assistants chosen primarily for their size and strength."[14] Legal commentator Terri Siegel explains:

> *A variety of techniques are applied, all aimed at forcing a rejection of the new religious beliefs. To reduce resistance, the deprogrammer's subject may be denied food and sleep, while the deprogrammers propose a barrage of questions regarding the cult's [sic] beliefs and practices. This is to demonstrate inconsistencies which deprogrammers claim exist in the theology of many religious cults. Attacks are made on the motives of cult leaders for their use of members to amass wealth, and for grief caused to parents and family by virtue of the cultist's devotion. The successful completion of this phase of deprogramming generally produces a docile, lifeless and frightened individual who has completely rejected any religious affiliation.*[15]

One of the most influential books endorsing deprogramming as the cure for "brainwashing" is *Snapping* by Flo Conway and Jim Siegelman.[16] This book is used as the major reference source for deprogrammers during their "dialogue" or interrogation of religious adherents. As Lowell Streiker explains, "If Lifton's *Thought Reform and the Psychology of Totalism* is deprogramming's Bible, *Snapping* is its Summa Theologica, Constitution, and Encyclopedia Britannica all rolled into one!"[17]

This book has served to impress many victims of deprogramming as authentic evidence that they have been subjected to a "sudden personality change." Conway and Siegelman assert that "mind-altering" techniques such as repetition of chants, intimate touching, physical duress, etc. tamper with the quality of information fed into the brain leading to "information disease." The book has been particularly effective with the deprogramming victim who is totally isolated and has no way of verifying the truth of Conway and Siegelman's theory. However, for the record, this book has been severely discredited by both social scientists and psychiatrists such as James R. Lewis,[18] David Bromley,[19] Brock Kilbourne, [20] and Lowell Streiker. Streiker finds it difficult to contain his contempt for this book largely because the elaborate theory about "information disease" that Conway and Siegelman have created applies to just about any activity, particularly if there is any intensity in it at all. As Streiker remarks, "Anything which reaches above the threshold of boredom is suspect." He concludes, "Obviously there is a whole lot of brainwashing going on, and very little of it by the handful of religious sects routinely lambasted by the ACN [Anti-Cult Network]."[21]

James Lewis and Brock Kilbourne also offer harsh criticism of the Conway and Siegelman conclusions. Based on his study, social psychologist Kilbourne critiques the lack of statistical support for the "information disease" hypothesis.[22] Lewis, on the basis of his extensive research, confirms this, pointing out that "the trauma of the shattering of one's religious faith (such as occur during deprogramming)—rather then 'cultic mind control'—are responsible for 'information disease'."[23] Kilbourne concludes: "What is perhaps more surprising than the Conway and Siegelman conclusions about the destructive effects of cults in the absence of supporting data is the almost blind endorsement by some of their study on cults (see the *Collegiate Advisor,* December '82, January '83, p.17). Such pseudo-scientific research may tell us more about some who study cults than about the cults themselves."[24]

There are many individuals who have engaged in the shady practice of deprogramming, among them Ted Patrick, Joe Alexander, Sr., Joe Alexander, Jr., Galen Kelly (who will be referred to in Chapter 8), Robert Brandyberry, Ken Connor,

Ford Greene, Neil Maxwell and many others. Many of them have been criminally convicted for their activities. Perhaps the most notorious is Ted Patrick. He is considered the "father of deprogramming," and in his book *Let Our Children Go!* he verifies these incredible accounts of the deprogramming process. He told one victim, "I can stay here three, four months. Even longer. Nobody's going anywhere." He admits to using "mace" on people who try to interfere with his work, limiting the sleep of the victim, hiring thugs to help him carry out his kidnappings and using physical violence.[25]

Where do deprogrammers get the authority to make these cosmic judgments about religious sects? What qualifications do they have to judge persons as "brainwashed" or to apply dangerous methods of enforced behavior modification? One might ask if this is a group of professionally trained psychiatrists, theologians, or social scientists? No. For example, as Le Moult points out, Ted Patrick "says he is a high school dropout. His only training appears to be a working knowledge of the Christian Bible. There is no evidence that he knows anything about eastern religions. Nor are there indications that other deprogrammers are qualified to make judgments about the mind, the soul [or] God."[26]

From personal contact with Patrick, Lowell Streiker bluntly states: "I found Ted Patrick the most programmed individual I had ever met." Streiker adds: "I felt that I was dealing with a fast-talking quick-buck artist with little understanding of the depths of human psychology or of religious experience. *He is definitely antireligious.* He told me that the Bible is the most brainwashing book ever written."[27]

In his audacious book, Patrick confirms the legitimacy that psychiatry has lent to "deprogramming" efforts when describing the kidnapping of a young man, Wes Lockwood, whose Catholic parents had hired Patrick because they disapproved of their son's allegiance to a Pentecostal Missionary Fellowship. Once they had forced their victim into the car, they proceeded down the turnpike but were stopped by the Highway patrol when their unusual behavior—a struggling Wes—was observed at the toll booth. Patrick describes what happened:

> *We were surrounded by troopers armed with rifles, shotguns, pistols, all pointed at us...We crawled out, very carefully and spreadeagled ourselves against the car while the troopers frisked us for weapons. Then they demanded our identification.* ***Fortunately Lockwood (Wes's father) was carrying a letter from the Yale Psychiatric Department and this had a most dramatic softening effect on the attitude of the troopers.****(emphasis added)*[28]

The victim's father had a letter from a psychiatrist describing Wes's "unhealthy mental state," although there was *no* indication that the psychiatrist had even seen or examined Wes.[29]

The sworn testimonies of people who have been victimized by kidnapping and attempted faithbreaking read like bizarre tales from the Spanish inquisition. The following is a statement from Walter Taylor, Jr., a monk of an Old Catholic Order:

> *I was taken from my residence, the Monastery of the Holy Protection of the Blessed Virgin Mary...Oklahoma City, on July 15,1972, and by court order...was put under a temporary guardianship of my father, Dr. Walter Taylor. This proceeding was without notice and no fair hearing was held and the attorney of my choice, Charles E. Lane, was excluded from the courtroom on the grounds that he was a member of the same religious group. The purpose of all this was to deny me the right to practice the religion of my choice—Old Catholicism.*
>
> *I was taken to Akron, Ohio, by plane where I was kept in a motel room by a goon squad...My monastic clothes were ripped off me while four persons held me down. My crucifix was taken away from me. I was harassed for thirteen hours by various persons working in shifts. I was kept awake and not permitted to sleep...I was ridiculed and harassed about the religious practice of mentally calling on the name of Jesus as a prayer. I was threatened with commitment to a mental institution if I did not cooperate and renounce my religion....My captors bragged that they had participated in taking 300 persons*

> *from religious groups for 'deprogramming' and that only the last 50 cases had been by legal means....I was kept at [deprogrammer] Mr. Howard's house in Mesa, Arizona....Mr. Howard discussed his sexual exploits and fornications and encouraged me to have sexual intercourse, which is contrary to my monastic beliefs.*[30]

Bromley and Shupe assert: "Deprogrammers are self-serving, illegal, and fundamentally immoral. In some cases, despite their protests to the contrary, they have profited handsomely from this practice."[31] Dean Kelley also condemns this practice which he refers to as "protracted spiritual gang-rape until they yield their most cherished religious commitments." He urges that it be prosecuted even more vigorously than any other kidnapping because "it strikes at the most precious and vulnerable portion of the victim's life, religious convictions and commitments."[32]

Former Unification Church member Chris Elkins, who himself left the church through deprogramming, expressed his view that "deprogramming leaves God out of the situation." Furthermore, in his book *What Do You Say To A Moonie?* he states, "it aborts the search for truth" by the adherent, often leading to severe psychological and emotional damage to its victims.[33]

In a recent article, "Ted Patrick and the Development of Deprogramming," Bromley offers a detailed analysis of Ted Patrick's philosophy and rationale for his deprogramming activities on the basis of viewing many hours of videotapes of Patrick's actual deprogramming sessions. He explains how Patrick perceives entry into a religious group. As Patrick describes it, the first contact involves making eye contact and initiating a conversation on some subject of mutual interest. The ulterior objective here is to get the individual thinking in a single frame of mind. This corresponds to an unconscious state which, Patrick asserts, most normal individuals are in 30% of the time. One example he uses frequently as an illustration is driving through Los Angeles and not being able to remember stopping at traffic lights because he was in an unconscious state of mind.[34]

Once this initial eye contact has been made, the cult member can place the individual in a complete trance without, supposedly, the individual's knowledge or permission. According to Patrick, this capacity physically comes from brainwaves which are projected outward through the cult member's eyes and fingertips. The individual's mind then switches from conscious to unconscious and a post-hypnotic suggestion is in place. Patrick asserts that the more "brilliant" individuals are more easily hypnotized.[35]

Patrick apparently believes that this is the beginning of the brainwashing process and that through the subsequent lectures and workshops a new recruit picks up a cult-imposed personality. In fact, as Bromley explains, Patrick regards members of new religions as literally possessed, constantly referring to deprogrammees as mindless robots and zombies. Patrick also asserts that brainwashing has reduced them to less than two years old mentally and that, in his opinion, they no longer have the capacity to distinguish right from wrong.[36]

Bromley's overall evaluation of Patrick is as follows:

> *He sees the concept of mind control so broadly that it would seem to lack any concrete meaning. For example, he states that he was programmed by his parents and that programming children properly is a parental responsibility. He reports that he programmed himself through overzealously reading the Bible. He contends that Satan used mind control on Eve in the Garden of Eden to induce Eve to eat the forbidden fruit. He asserts that communist states are able to use mind control to totally control their citizenry. In this connection, he observes that if leaders in China want ping pong players, they simply program them from birth. And he refers to China as a whole nation of mindless robots. He alleges that the widespread practice among pentecostal/charismatic Christians of speaking in tongues is simply self-hypnosis...He even contends that he was induced by mind control techniques to purchase a vacuum cleaner he did not want from a door to door salesman, and that Billy Graham mesmerizes people over television. The concept of mind control reflected in these diverse practices, real and mythological, is so broad and vague as to lack useful meaning. The only consistent feature of the concept as Patrick employs it is that the contents or outcomes involved are undesirable from his perspective.*[37]

It should be noted that Ted Patrick, although recognized as the first person to begin the practice of deprogramming or faithbreaking, is not entirely typical of all deprogrammers. Patrick is known for the use of violence, physical abuse and confrontational tactics, but there are others who are more careful to avoid some of these tactics. Some have been subtle in the way that adherents are abducted or held captive. The victims have sometimes been told that they are free to leave, but when they attempt to do so, they discover they are not free at all; they are captives.

In recent years, following numerous convictions for kidnapping and false imprisonment as well as the severe disrepute they have received, some deprogrammers have developed new terminology to get people to leave various religions. One term that is frequently used is "exit counseling," which professes to be "non-coercive deprogramming" and has an emphasis on getting the member away from the group for lengthy conversations.[38] According to Lowell Streiker, the term "exit counseling" is often used to misrepresent the true intent, which is usually coercive deprogramming involving forced incarceration.[39] Even in those instances where no direct coercion is involved, the ultimate purpose does not amount to an exchange of views or "dialogue" in any real sense. The deprogrammer has one purpose in mind—to decimate the beliefs of the adherent (of any faith) and to replace them with his concept of "truth."

Gordon Melton and Robert Moore in their book *The Cult Experience* describe the kind of "dialogue" involved:

> *More often than not, the dialogue takes the form of an intense interrogation, with several people taking turns engaging the cult member in a session of diatribe, badgering, leading questions, and theological and biblical dialectics. Few persons of any faith would be able to counter all the arguments that could be brought against the practices of their faith, and few cultists are informed enough to understand the rationale for all their group's rituals and beliefs. Isolated and surrounded by deprogrammers, the individual faces intellectual attacks on her or his belief system, ridicule of unusual patterns of behavior, and the continual presentation of symbols of the benefits of the life that was left to join the group. The net result of all the practices of the deprogrammer is to wear down the cult member's resistance to accepting the deprogrammers' views. The practices cause physical*

> *and emotional fatigue and create a strong sense of humiliation and guilt. The controlled environment produces a sense of hopelessness. Cut off from the group, the confined individual is alone. Eventually, the wearing down prepares the imprisoned member for the presentation of a way out: "Conversion" to the deprogrammers' world view and acceptance of the deprogrammers' goal.*[40]

How Faith Can Be Broken

One may wonder how it is possible for the adherent of any religious faith to have his or her faith broken. One key reason is that it is far easier to destroy a person's faith and trust than it is to help a person become a trusting, caring, inspired and dedicated individual. Why is this so? Simply put, everyone has been let down, disappointed and violated in some way. Most people's trust has been broken, often with some very deep scars remaining. We live in a world where we are often taught not to trust anyone—"just look out for number one." This advice comes from adults—adults who are not evil or badly motivated—but who are genuinely concerned about the well-being of their sons and daughters in a sometimes cruel and difficult world.

Futhermore, to a person who has not studied this issue, it may be difficult to comprehend how deeply committed members of religious groups could somehow suddenly be turned around to the point where they become deprogrammers or faithbreakers themselves. In effect, the faithbreaking process is a form of counter-conversion, a system of behavior modification intended to change the victim's beliefs and make him conform to religious beliefs and practices that are acceptable to his parents. From his study of the issue, legal writer John Le Moult concluded that deprogramming is "far more like brainwashing than the conversion process by which members join sects. The restraint, deprivation of sleep, constant talk, denunciation, alternation of tough and easy talk, emotional appeals and incessant questioning finally cause a *break* in the will giving the deprogrammer a certain power over the victim."[41]

Sociologist James T. Richardson agrees with this perspective. He concludes his study, "Conversion, Brainwashing, and Deprogramming in New Religious Groups," with this statement: "Those who engage in or support deprogramming assume a large responsibility to demonstrate that their 'solution' is not worse than the alleged problem of membership in new religious groups. And given the weight of evidence from scholars in the field, proving that point will be difficult indeed."[42]

Parents' Reactions

One may also wonder how parents ever become involved in such an outrageous abuse of their adult child. However, based on the widely circulated horror stores of life in a "cult," it is not surprising that parents have been willing to take drastic action. For parents to suddenly discover that their precious son or daughter has been caught up in some "weird" cult, following some "strange" Oriental or Indian guru, comes as a severe shock. Immediately the parents wonder where they went wrong. Somehow the conversion to this "far out" religion is interpreted as the worst possible thing that could happen to their son or daughter. Addiction to drugs, alcohol or premarital sex is at least tolerable, but "my son a Moonie—good God, NO!"

Fortunately, most parents trust their adult children and are willing to investigate and try to understand what they are doing. Furthermore, they realize they cannot choose their offspring's way of life, and should respect their ideals and beliefs. However, some parents have felt obliged to intervene forcibly, largely due to the hysteria created by sensationalist media and by professional faithbreakers who prey on innocent but terrified parents, feeding their worst fears with outrageous tales of "mind control," food and sleep deprivation, "zombies," and so forth.

On the basis of these fears, some parents have been encouraged by faithbreakers to hire them and to lure their adult son or daughter into a position where he or she can be kidnapped, using outright deception, rationalized by the belief that "the end justifies the means." This is not to say that the motivation of these parents is anything but sincere and genuine. Nevertheless, the fear instilled in them causes them to violate a very important principle: the fundamental right of an adult to believe as he or she chooses. Countless people have sacrificed their lives to uphold this freedom. As Dean Kelley writes:

> *The meaning of true liberty, especially religious liberty, is that persons must be free to subject their reason to the demands of faith if they want to do so, however bizarre and unreasonable that faith may seem to others. People must be free to live out other understandings of the good life than those accepted by conventional society if they want to do so.*[43]

Civil rights attorney Jeremiah S. Gutman, past president of the New York Civil Liberties Union, suggests that if people in this country think it is all right to lock up a person just because of disapproval of what he believes, their approach is indistinguishable from the Soviets' treatment of dissidents. He suspects that this society is attempting more and more to deal with its non-conformists by declaring them to be "batty" and thereby feeling justified in locking them up "for their own good." At a symposium on this subject reported in the *Review of Law and Social Change,* Gutman added, "If I want to join a group (whether it is denominated a 'religion' or not), I am free to do so. I am guaranteed that right under the freedom of association clause of the First Amendment. Some may not think it is good for me. Some may convince me not to do it. I may listen to these arguments but I may also turn my back and walk away as I choose. *I cannot be forced to listen.* My right to associate freely cannot be hindered, so long as I do not conspire to commit crimes..."[44]

A Personal Account

In addition to compiling research and interviews on the subject of deprogramming, this author had the unfortunate but revealing opportunity to draw on first-hand experience with this phenomenon.

My parents had been rather shocked by my conversion to the Unification Church. I had been fairly serious about religion all of my life (except for a two-year period of agnosticism between the ages of 20-22). I attended church regularly, prayed twice daily and read a chapter of the Bible each day. My parents knew that I went to church, but they were not fully aware that there was a tremendous struggle going on inside my heart. In the year preceding my conversion to the Unification Church I prayed over and over for guidance from God as to how I could find fulfillment, how I could serve Him. I felt unfulfilled in law school, and I did not believe I could find real contentment in worldly concepts of success.[45] My parents were easy prey for faithbreakers because of a combination of not knowing what I was going through internally, not knowing anything about the Unification movement, and not trusting the information I sent to them.

As good parents, they were naturally concerned about my welfare. They were alarmed by terrifying tales about what the "Moonies" might do to their son, and they felt compelled to intervene. Unfortunately, they overlooked one very important consideration—perhaps their son *did* know what he was doing. Maybe he had experienced a real conversion. The faithbreakers, however, had terrified them so much that they reacted impulsively. They did not take the initial step of investigating for themselves. When a parent receives a visit by such zealous faithbreakers, the natural response is: "How can I get my child out?" The "professional thugs" have the right answer: "We can...for a 'small' price." Thus, these "Guns for Hire" take the law, the life and the ideals of the adult victim into their own hands. They promise to become the heroic "saviors" and then proceed to abduct.

It is important to note that I had made efforts to explain what I was doing through lengthy telephone calls, through sending church literature, and so forth. But because of the heavy propaganda my parents had received, it became impossible to convince them that I was not "brainwashed." They had been persuaded not to trust or believe anything I said. In my honest opinion, if there is such a thing, it was *they* who had actually been "brainwashed." This fact was borne out when I was actually kidnapped—four months after joining the Unification Church. When my mother first saw me, she was extremely surprised and pleased that I appeared quite normal. It led her to exclaim as she squeezed my hand and gave me a hug, "John, you look good!" In fact, as soon as she became supportive of statements I made to the faithbreakers, she was forced to leave the room, despite my pleadings that she remain with me.

My former employer, who was then a Cabinet Minister in Canadian Prime Minister Pierre Trudeau's government and who had arranged my abduction, had been more thoroughly "brainwashed" by the hysteria generated by the faithbreakers.[46] After seeing me, he asserted that I was but a "shell of my former self." That was after I was unwilling to agree with his viewpoint about the Unification Church.[47]

During the time I was held against my will in a Northern California motel room, I was verbally attacked, berated, insulted, and threatened with weeks or months of further incarceration and abuse if I did not recant my faith. In a word, I was terrified. Without a doubt, it was the most terrifying experience of my entire life. It is one thing for one's physical life to be endangered, but it is much more serious to have one's spiritual beliefs and ideals subjected to such an assault as I encountered during this faithbreaking process.

In between the insults and abuse, I was told that my abductors were only interested in asking questions about the Unification Church so they could "find out what it was all about." Perhaps the most significant and revealing exchange during my abduction came when, after continued questioning and harassment, I offered to invite one of the local Unification Church leaders to come to answer some of their questions since there were many aspects of the movement with which I was not yet familiar, having joined only four months previously. My request was not even considered. They simply refused, betraying their entire pretense of sincerity. They had no desire whatsoever to "learn" about my beliefs nor to "understand" what I was doing. They simply wanted to crush my beliefs.

It was after this kind of "dialogue" that I realized it was impossible to persuade them that I had made a reasoned and conscious decision to join the Unification movement. As soon as this became apparent to me, I realized that somehow I had to escape. It was clear that they would not accept me as I was, and I was aware that my faith could possibly be broken if I was placed under prolonged emotional and psychological pressure. I felt that almost anyone in my situation could conceivably have their faith broken. I was honestly not capable at that time of answering all of their loaded questions about Rev. Moon and the movement. I did not know Rev. Moon personally; I had not yet met him, and though I was profoundly moved by his teachings, I was not fully knowledgeable of his ministry. I knew that the seed of doubt is always much easier to plant than the seed of trust, so I wanted to learn all of the background on Rev. Moon and the Unification Church on my own terms, not under such oppressive circumstances. I had to escape.

As a result of my "obstinacy" and unwillingness to engage in this one-sided "dialogue" with the deprogrammers, everyone became rather nervous, especially after I made an attempt to escape. They had good reason to be nervous given that there was a Canadian Cabinet Minister, his Executive Assistant, a Vice-Consul from the Canadian Consulate in San Franscisco and three deprogrammers holding me captive in the Best Western Motel in Corte Madera, California. They decided to take me out of this motel and fly me to a "deprogramming center in the east" (I subsequently learned of their plans when I happened to see a file with my name on it). As it turned out, they let down their guard while changing planes at O'Hare Airport in Chicago which is when I was finally able to make a successful escape.

Since that time my parents have experienced a dramatic change in their viewpoint. Over the past nine years, they have shown great willingness to understand my lifestyle and the Unification movement as a whole. They have also acknowledged that their original opposition to my involvement in the Unification Church as well as their collaboration with deprogrammers was based on a tremendous amount of misinformation. Their biggest complaint has been the severely distorted impression they have received from the media, which had been multiplied by the faithbreakers who approached them.

There are many parents who have this feeling of regret. One couple who had tried to "deprogram" their daughter write that they

> *now realize that deprogramming is a degrading, dehumanizing, thoroughly evil practice that is being done by unprofessional opportunists that exploit parents' love for children. Any attempt to make deprogramming legal should be opposed by all right-thinking people, and parents who are considering hiring a deprogrammer to supposedly rescue their adult child from an organization with which they are not thoroughly familiar through their own research, and are relying on what others have told them, should stop and think twice before doing this terrible thing. Parenting is the most difficult job in the world. But if parents have raised their children with eternal values of honesty, integrity, love, compassion, respect and love for God, parents and family, then those parents should have enough faith in their adult children to take their word against the word of anyone else, and should respect their adult child's ability to make his or her own decisions.*[48]

During recent visits, it has been readily apparent that my parents are very relieved to see that my life is one of dedication to a pure and very traditional religious ideal—the creation of a world of love centered on God. I can also sense their pride in what I am doing. Following one of their visits, I remarked to my wife that they had never really expressed their pride in what I was doing before I joined this movement, even though I had previously achieved some substantial level of success. I sense this is because they now hold a respect for my commitment to my ideals and a life of faith that they never saw in me before.

These experiences with my family have demonstrated to me the result of maintaining one's own faith in a profound ideal, in the face of great oppostion and difficulty. In spite of my parents' initial reservations, it has become increasingly apparent to them that my beliefs are very rational, reasonable and indeed well-founded. Even more importantly, they have seen that this belief system and lifestyle have made their son a better person.

Aside from the importance of maintaining faith in my ideals, I must stress that this reconciliation would not have been possible without my parents' renewed efforts to understand what I was doing as well as their tremendous love and respect for me. I feel a deep love and gratitude to them for this, and I believe that it is on a basis of such openness and mutual respect that all church members and their parents can resolve any misunderstanding or fear they might have.

An Historical Perspective

Based on such experiences as these, critics have alleged that the Unification Church creates a breakdown in family relationships. However, the reality is quite different, especially when placed in the context of history. In his article, "Deprogramming and Religious Liberty," Dean Kelley confronts this point. He makes reference to a passage of the New Testament which is not easy to accept although it may shed some light on the difficulties that arise in responding to the prophetic message:

> *Do not think that I have come to bring peace on earth; I have come not to bring peace, but a sword. For I have come to set a man against his father, and a daughter against her mother, and a daughter-in-law against her mother-in-law and a man's foes will be those of his own household. He who loves father or mother more than me is not worthy of me; and he who loves son or daughter more than me is not worthy of me, and he who does not take up his cross and follow me is not worthy of me.*[49]

Kelley points out:

> *These words, attributed to Jesus, do not fall graciously upon the ear. People seem to have difficulty remembering them. Yet, there is no truer description of the perils of conversion...Giovanni Bernadone lived in the twelfth century, son of a successful businessman. When he sold some cloth from his father's warehouse to rebuild a ruined church, the elder Bernadone took him to the local bishop to disinherit him. At that moment he removed all of his clothes, returned them to his father and went on his way in a monk's cloak to pursue his religious convictions. History now remembers him as St. Francis of Assisi—instead of the prosperous textile merchant he could have become.*[50]

To keep things in perspective, the scenario described does not apply to the relationship between the vast majority of Unification Church members and their parents. In fact, many members have developed much closer relationships with their families because of their experience in the Unification movement. This is based on Church teaching which emphasizes the eternal bonds that exist in all family relationships as well as the importance of respect and care for elders. It might also be added that in recent years Church leaders have explicitly urged members to resolve difficulties that may have existed in the past. This restorative process becomes far, far easier when members can be assured that they will not be abucted and subjected to the trauma of faithbreaking.

Furthermore, (as more fully explained in Chapter 9) the confrontation and tension that sometimes arises between parents and their "reborn" child is not sought by the Unification movement. The teaching of Rev. Moon stresses the absolute importance of the strong God-centered family unit as the basis or core of a healthy society. It is essential, therefore, to understand that the root cause of the hysteria that has led to the entire deprogramming phenomenon does not necessarily lie with the new movement itself.

Theologian Frank Flinn concludes his recent article "Criminalizing Conversion" on this same note:

> *Perhaps it is time for Americans to consult the light of history for a longer view of enlightened opinion. This era is not the first time that conversion has created controversy. The young adults who joined the medieval urban youth movement known as the mendicant order—such as the Dominicans, Franciscans and Augustinians—were called* ***dementes*** *("insane") and* ***filii diaboli*** *("sons of the devil") by clerics of the establishment.*
>
> *Both St. Francis of Assisi and St. Thomas Aquinas were kidnapped and imprisoned by their parents and relatives who tried to "deprogram" them out of their bizarre beliefs and lifestyles as "mendicants," i.e., beggars. Similar charges and epithets were hurled by the established Harvard divines against the principals and participants in the Great Awakening. I will leave it to the reader as to whether or not St. Francis, St. Thomas and Jonathan Edwards were a boon to the spiritual history of humanity. For those who take time to consult the light of history there is the illuminating fact that the first treatise against "conservatorship" and "deprogramming" on religious grounds was written by St. Thomas himself. It was called, in Latin, Contra pestiferam doctrinam retrahentium homines a religionis ingressu*—"Against the Pernicious Teaching of Those Dragging Youth Away from Entering the Religious Life."[51]

References

1. During the late 1970's, the number of Unification Church members who were subjected to "deprogramming" was several hundred each year. During the 1980's, the number has decreased dramatically. In 1985, the total number of cases reported was less than one dozen.

2. See description of research by Dr. Saul Levine, "Report on Physical and Mental Health Aspects of Religious Cults and Mind Bending Groups," cited in Daniel Hill, *Study of Mind Development Groups, Sects and Cults in Ontario: A Report to the Ontario Government* (Toronto: The Queen's Printer, 1980) 703.

3. John E. Le Moult, "Deprogramming Members of Religious Sects," *Fordham Law Review* Vol. 46, 1978, 599. This was recently cited with approval by the United States Court of Appeals for the Second Circuit in *Colombrito v. Kelly*, 764 F.2d 122, 125 (2nd Cir. 1985). This case is explained in detail in Chapter 8.

4. *Kelley, "Deprogramming and Religious Liberty," Civil Liberties Review,* Vol. 4, July/Aug. 1977, 27. *See also:* Note—"Conservatorships and Religious Cults: Divining a Theory of Free Exercise," *New York University Law Review*, Vol. 53, 1978, 1289.

5. "And Now-Deprogramming of Christians is Taking Place," *Christianity Today*, April 22, 1983. This article describes the kidnapping of Betsy and Whitney Chase in an effort to force them to renounce their involvement with the Assemblies of God (a Pentecostal denomination). The article noted: "Eyebrows are raising now that Christians have become fair game in the deprogrammers' market. Recently Ted Patrick asserted that Jerry Falwell has more people under mind control than [Sun Myung] Moon and that 'Falwell leads the biggest cult in the nation.' The incident in Detroit is not the only one. Christians who belong to the San Francisco-based Jews for Jesus are sometimes victims. This year there have been at least four incidents in which Jews for Jesus street missionaries in New York City have been assaulted by the militant

Jewish Defense League. In 1981, a Soviet Jew from Chicago who had become a Christian was kidnapped and taken to New York for deprogramming.... Deprogramming has also plagued Maranatha Campus Ministries, a charismatic ministry represented on more than 60 college campuses in 32 states. Maranatha's director of missions, Ted Doss, knows of at least 10 incidents of attempted deprogramming of students belonging to Maranatha." Ibid. See also Thomas Robbins, "'Uncivil Religions' and Religious Deprogramming," *Thought, Fordham University Quarterly,* Vol. LXI, June 1986, 278.

6. *Eilers v. Coy,* 582 F. Supp. 1093 (E.D. Minn. 1984).

7. The case of Stephanie Riethmiller who was kidnapped and held for one week to reverse her lesbian attachment to another woman, *Time,* May 3, 1982, "Deprogramming Tied to Kidnap of Local Woman," *The Cincinnati Post* (Cincinnati, Ohio), Oct. 17, 1981.

8. Kelley, supra, 27

9. *Philadelphia Enquirer,* August 17, 1980, 1. See also William Rusher, "Don't Like Someone's Views? Deprogram Him," *New York Tribune* (New York, N.Y.), May 27, 1983.

10. Conversation with detective Alfred Matteoni of the San Francisco Police Department (March, 1981).

11. Terri Siegel, "Deprogramming Religious Cultists," *Loyola of Los Angeles Law Review,* Vol. 11, 1978, 812.

12. Le Moult, supra, 603. For detailed description by deprogrammer Ted Patrick of his abduction of members of religious sects, see Patrick and Dulack, *Let Our Children Go!* (New York: Ballantine, 1976) 73-74, 95-102.

13. Examples of actual situations include an abandoned Texas ranch house, a house on the Alberta prairies and a cottage on the shores of Lake Ontario in upstate New York.

14. Siegel, supra, 813.

15. Ibid., 813-14.

16. Flo Conway and Jim Siegelman, *Snapping: America's Epidemic of Sudden Personality Change* (New York: Delta, 1979). Since writing this book, Conway and Siegelman have turned their anti-religious rhetoric against fundamentalist Christians asserting that they are more dangerous than the "destructive cults." See also Flo Conway and Jim Siegelman, *Holy Terror* (New York: Doubleday, 1982) 5.

17. Streiker, supra, 163.

18. James R. Lewis, "'Information Disease,' and the Legitimization of Religious Repression," supra.

19. James R. Lewis & David G. Bromley, "The Cult Withdrawal Syndrome: A Case of Misattrition of Cause?" 18. Forthcoming in the *Journal for the Scientific Study of Religion,* Sept. 1987

20. Brock K. Kilbourne, "The Conway and Siegelman Claims Against Religious Cults: An Assessment of Their Data," *Journal For the Scientific Study of Religion,* Vol. 22, No. 4, Dec., 1983, 380.

21. Streiker, supra, 166. Streiker quotes from the back cover of the paperback edition as an indictment in itself: "Hare Krishna chanters, est graduates, Moonies, Born Again converts...Charles Colson, Eldridge Cleaver, Patty Hearst, "Son of Sam"—What can they all possibly have in common? The answer is "snapping"—the term Flo Conway and Jim Siegelman use to describe the sudden drastic alteration of personality that has become an American phenomenon in the past decade and is spreading fast. According to Conway and Siegelman, snapping is visible among religious-cult members, today's popular self-improvement mass therapies, and even within the vast Evangelical movement. The authors point out that mind-altering techniques employed by

these groups tamper with the kind and quality of information fed to the brain—through isolation, repetition of chants, monotonous music, intimate touching, lack of sleep, physical duress, and fatigue." Ibid., 164.

22. Kilbourne, supra, 384.

23. Lewis, "Information Disease," supra, 6.

24. Kilbourne, supra, 384.

25. Le Moult, supra, 604.

26. Ibid., 605. Shupe and Bromley add: "Deprogrammers such as Ted Patrick and Joe Alexander have no special qualifications in psychology or psychiatry. Their "calling" appears to have flowed more from inspiration and, some have alleged, from the short-run profitability of deprogramming. At the same time, such pseudoprofessionals claim a monopoly on the skills of understanding and neutralizing evil. For example, in their recent book, *Let Our Children Go!,* Ted Patrick and Tom Dulack immodestly assessed his abilities to a parent before a deprogramming in this way (1976, p. 82): "Please try to understand this: I haven't found a psychiatrist, or any attorney, or a doctor or anyone else who knows anything about brainwashing and mind control." Anson D. Shupe and David G. Bromley, "Witches, Moonies, and Accusations of Evil," in Robbins and Anthony (eds.), *In Gods We Trust,* supra, 257.

27. Streiker, *Mind-Bending,* supra, 39.

28. Ted Patrick with Tom Dulack, *Let Our Children Go,* supra, 93-100.

29. Ibid.

30. *Affadavit of Walter Robert Taylor, Jr.*, filed August 12, 1976, Oklahoma City, (Retained in author's files). See also a more detailed description by the United States Court of Appeals for the Tenth Circuit in *Taylor v. Gilmartin,* 686 F.2d 1346, 1348-50 (10th Cir. 1982).

31. Bromley & Shupe, *Strange Gods,* supra, 204. See also "Resolution on Deprogramming," adopted by the National Council of Churches, Feb. 28, 1974.

32. Dean Kelley, supra, 32.

33. Chris Elkins, *What Do You Say To a Moonie?* (Wheaton, IL: Tyndale House, 1981) 88-90.

34. David G. Bromley, "Ted Patrick and the Development of Deprogramming," presented at the 1985 Annual Meeting of the Society for the Scientific Study of Religion.

35. Ibid., 10.

36. Ibid.

37. Ibid., 8-9.

38. James T. Richardson, "Conversion, Brainwashing, and Deprogramming in New Religious Groups," 13-14. See note 42 below. See also Bromley, "Ted Patrick" supra, 4-5.

39. Lowell Streiker, interview, August 14, 1986.

40. Melton and Moore, supra, 78-79. See also Le Moult, supra, 606-7.

41. Le Moult, supra, 606-7.

42. James T. Richardson, "Conversion, Brainwashing and Deprogramming in New Religious Groups," presented to faculty of Free University of Amsterdam, May 1, 1981, published in *Religiuze Bewegingen in Nederland,* 15.

43. Dean Kelley, supra, 30.

44. Jeremiah S. Gutman, "Extemporaneous Remarks," *Review of Law and Social Change,* Vol. 9, 1980-81, 70-71.

45. A recent *New York Times* article points out that many "successful people are becoming troubled, conflicted, or emotionally damaged by their work and career climb." Psychotherapists say that many "successful" people feel they have been encouraged to betray their deepest values and ideals in order to attain "success" leading to severe emotional and psychological problems. See "The Strange Agony of Success," *The New York Times* (New York, N.Y.), Sunday, Aug. 24, 1986, F-1. See also "After a Year, Grave Doubts Begin to Rise," *The National Law Journal,* Sept. 8, 1986, 6.

46. See, e.g., "Former Cafik Aide Returns to Unification Church," *The Sault Star* (Sault Ste. Marie, Ontario,) Jan. 8, 1978; "Former Aide Claims Cafik Held Him Against His Will," *The Daily Mercury* (Guelph, Ontario), Jan. 18, 1978; "Did Cafik Imprison Moonie?", *Ottawa Today* (Ottawa, Canada), Jan. 19, 1978. See also Bart Testa, "Making Crime Seem Natural: The Press and Deprogramming" in *A Time for Consideration,* supra, 80, n.1.

47. To be fair to Mr. Cafik, it must be acknowledged that he risked his career to "get me out of the Moonies." Apparently Prime Minister Trudeau had told him not to participate in this affair, but because of our friendship he took the risk. Therefore, despite his unwillingness to respect my freedom to make my own decision, or to take the time to investigate the beliefs and practices of the Unification Church from an objective point of view, I bear no anger or resentment towards him for the actions he took.

48. Sworn statement by Francis and Lorraine Duxbury, April 16, 1984, 3-4. (Retained in author's files.)

49. Matthew, 10:34-38.

50. Kelley, supra, 28.

51. Frank Flinn, "Criminalizing Conversion: The Legislative Assault on New Religions *et al.* ," 35. Forthcoming in James Day and William Laufer (eds.),*Crimes, Values and Religions* (Norwood, N.J.: Ablex, 1986).

Chapter 5

EX-MEMBERS

One of the major sources of criticism against new religious groups has been from former members who, for one reason or another have become disenchanted and thereafter tell their stories to the public. Books have been written on this subject; exposes have appeared in major newspapers; documentaries have been shown on probably every television network in the United States as well as in many other countries; movies have been produced;[1] and speaking tours have been arranged on high school and college campuses throughout America and elsewhere.

The stories that have been told have covered the spectrum from extreme bitterness and hostility to rather passive, resigned reflections on past experiences. Perhaps most noteworthy of all is the little known fact that the "silent majority" of those who have left new religious movements remain generally neutral or positive and feel grateful for their experiences.[2] In a study of forty-five ex-members of three controversial new religious movements including the Unification Church, Stuart Wright of the Center for Urban Church Studies in Nashville concludes:

> *Responses of voluntary defectors indicate that most assimilate their experiences in a constructive way and learn from them. In much the same way that individuals learn from any major social and psychological transition—whether it be from a career change, a divorce, or leaving the Armed services to re-enter civilian life—one can use these past experiences, events, and perceptions to build or guide future actions, to set different goals, and to establish new convictions. Moreover, a finding which clearly emerges from this data is the disconfirmation of any support for brainwashing. Regardless of how unproductive or unprofitable ex-members may envision their past involvement in a new religious movement, the overwhelming majority say they were participants by their own volition.*[3]

The fact is that nearly all of the hostility towards the Church has been engendered by those who were taken out by force, through the faithbreaking process. David Bromley refers to these as individuals who "have a strong interest in coloring their accounts."[4] Based on her widely-cited study, Trudy Solomon points out that those who leave various movements through deprogramming tend to adopt the brainwashing theories of conversion because of their contact with the anticult movement.[5] Wright's study confirms this finding. He reports that as a consequence of a forced exit, former members' accounts of their experience in new religious movements "are often infused with conspiratorial assumptions about 'mind control' and advanced techniques of psychological manipulation, generating what Shupe and Bromley(1980) have called 'atrocity tales.' One must seriously question, however, the validity of such explanations—particularly the language or conceptual framework of these accounts—when the respondents have undergone some type of deprogramming or comparable therapeutic treatment."[6]

The "atrocity tales" that Stuart Wright refers to are one of the ways that apostate or former members of any group attack their former allegiances. The term "apostate" is often used to refer to a particular kind of former member, one who renounces or turns against the group, whereas a "lapsed" member or "backslider" is someone who simply foregoes his former commitments. Due to the tremendous emotion involved, as when any relationship breaks down, there is good reason to question the authenticity of these "tales."

It should be noted that Unification Church members recognize that they have made mistakes as well. In his recent book, *To Bigotry, No Sanction,* Mose Durst, President of the Unification Church of America, devoted an entire chapter to this issue, "Mistakes in Building the Kingdom." He writes:

> *There have been many mistakes, but none of them malicious, devious, illegal, or intended to defraud, as our detractors charge. Rather, our mistakes are those made in youthful zeal and out of ignorance. Perhaps our mistakes are even understandable and forgivable, since no one has*

> *ever offered a course or written a book on how to found and establish a religion. Quite frankly, we had to learn about church-building through on-the-job training, by trial and error. I suspect that other religious pioneers have had the same experience.*[7]

However, there is still a great gap between, on the one hand, acknowledging that sometimes Church leaders have been overzealous in pushing their members in fundraising or in street evangelizing[8] and, on the other hand, the horrific tales that have been told by some ex-members. What accounts for these outrageous tales? Is the Unification Church really as terribly oppressive as some of these apostates would lead us to believe, or do they perhaps have an axe to grind? How does one account for the fact that most people who have any significant contact with the church, whether members or not, do not recognize in it the descriptions of the apostates?[9] Could it be that they are projecting into their recollections elements derived from the mythology of the anti-cult activists—in a manner similar to the tales of the infamous ex-nun Maria Monk?

Atrocity Tales are Nothing New

In a recent book which dealt with this issue, Catholic Sociologist Joseph Fichter writes that these tales from ex-members of the Unification Church are almost on a par with earlier atrocity stories that have been told by ex-priests and ex-nuns against the Catholic Church. He points out that the great majority of ex-members from any church quietly go their way. In many cases, they go with pleasant memories of their association, sometimes in bitterness, but with no determination to destroy their erstwhile comrades. In reality, it is a very small number of apostates who recount sordid anecdotes of their experience.[10]

Herbert Richardson did extensive research comparing the earlier anti-Catholic and anti-Semitic rhetoric with that against the Unification Church. His results are described in the chart on page 84. He suggests that one might ask if the very similarity in the patterns of these three anti-religious rhetorics should not make us suspect that "they are based more on primitive hatred than on empirical analysis?"[11]

Anti-Catholicism	*Anti-Semitism*	*Anti-Cultism*
The pope is seeking to take over the world.	The Jews are seeking to take over the world. (The Protocols of the Elders of Zion)	Moon is seeking to take over the world.
Catholicism is not a true religion, but a policital system.	Judaism is not a religion, but a political system.	The Unification Church is not a church but a political front group.
Catholics aren't loyal Americans, but are really loyal to Rome—a foreign power.	Jews aren't loyal Americans, but are really loyal to Israel.	Moon teaches Americans to fight for Korea.
The Catholic Church exploits the poor in order to build rich churches and buy land.	Jews are really only after money.	Moon claims to be a prophet, but is really only after profit.
The priests enslave the minds of young people, inculcating irrational superstition.	Judaism is a legalistic, tribalistic system, rituatlistic and anti-rational.	Moon brainwashes his converts.
Catholics control their young people's lives by teaching that sex is evil.	Jews control their young people's lives by making them feel guilty about marrying a non-Jew.	Moon controls young people's lives by making them remain chaste and then arranging their marriages.
Catholics justify lying by "mental reservation."	Jews always lie.	Moonies don't tell the truth but practice "heavenly deception."
Catholics entice children, while too young to decide for themselves, to become nuns and priests.	Jews kidnap gentile children for vile purposes.	Moon entices the young to leave their families.
Catholics are swarthy (Latin) and have too many children.	Jews have crooked noses and are verminous.	Moonies have glazed-eyes and are under-nourished.

Richardson writes that whenever he hears a Catholic person vilifying cultists, he is always reminded that, when young, he heard a Protestant fundamentalist describe Catholics in the same way. He says there was even a "converted Catholic priest" who came on a regular lecture circuit, describing how horribly the Catholic Church had held him by the mental chains of "superstition" until he was able to escape.[12*] Today "ex-cultists" travel the same circuit telling similar stories of how they were "mentally imprisoned" by Rev. Moon and others.[12] Richardson adds that whenever he has heard Rabbi James Rudin and others "vilifying the Moonies," he says he is "struck by the fact that what they are saying is exactly what Hitler said about the Jews."[13]

In an article entitled "Hammering the Heretics," Joseph Fichter comments that it "is as opprobrious now to be a Moonie as it was to be a Papist 150 years ago." Fichter questions whether we have forgotten the *Protocols of Zion* and the flood of anti-Semitic hate literature during the 1930's? He suggests that Roman Catholics ought to read Billington's *The Protestant Crusade* to remind themselves that they were targets of earlier persecution.[14]

The stories from ex-Mormons are remarkably similar to the allegations of hypnotic, trance-inducing influences of the new religions described by Ted Patrick in Chapter 4. In one tale by pseudo-apostate Maria Ward, *Female Life Among the Mormons,* the author described her capture in terms of "magnetic influence" and a "spell" being cast over her:

> *At this time I was wholly unacquainted with the doctrine of magnetic influence; but I soon became aware of some unaccountable power exercised over me by my fellow traveller. His presence seemed an irresistable fascination. His glittering eyes were fixed on mine; his breath fanned my cheek; I felt bewildered and intoxicated and partially lost the sense of consciousness, and the power of motion....I became immediately sensible of some unaccountable influence drawing my sympathies towards him. In vain I struggled to break the spell. I was like a fluttering bird before the gaze of the serpent-charmer.*[15]

In *Strange Gods,* Bromley and Shupe comment on the book *Crazy for God,* the autobiography of an ex-Unification Church member, Chris Edwards:

> *Aside from demonstrating a remarkable memory for details and events that allegedly occurred while his brain was being washed, Edwards' account of his indoctrination at the hands of the Unification Church's Oakland family is a modern illustration of a literary genre as old as the anti-Mormon and anti-Catholic movements of the early nineteenth century....With a literary style and deliberate melodramatic construction reminiscent of the script for a made-for-TV movie,* Crazy for God *makes one feel as if the ghost of Maria Monk, that self-proclaimed ex-nun from a nineteenth-century Montreal convent, had reappeared to promote another potboiler tract, this time substituting the Unification Church for the 'Papist' Roman Catholics.*[16]

The Impact of "Deprogramming" on Ex-Members

Ex-members of any group have a vested interest in explaining away their earlier "mistakes." This is amplified dramatically in the instance of a *forced* exit. Thus, as Bromley and Shupe observe, it is the victims of "deprogrammings" who have been manipulated into making public admissions of having been "brainwashed."

Numerous people who have gone through this terrifying experience have been forced to sign statements reciting the stereotypical allegations. Typical is a statement that "I had been under mind control and was happy to have been deprogrammed. When I refused to sign it, they threatened to keep me locked up."[17] Another typical example is: "They had me sign a release form stating that I had been deceived and manipulated by the Unification Church and that I was going to Virginia of my own free will. I only signed it because it seemed the only way to gain my freedom."[18] Another deprogramming victim was repeatedly urged to sign a statement that she had "been the victim of mind control through brainwashing."[19]

This practice is confirmed by Lowell Streiker who states, from his experience at his Freedom Counseling Center for former members of various groups, that he is aware of many instances where victims of deprogramming were given statements to sign with the usual allegations such as "I was under mind control."[20] Streiker also points out that deprogrammers such as Ted Patrick admit that they actually "program" members of the so-called "cults" into believing that they were brainwashed or under mind control. Streiker recounts that Patrick had personally described one deprogramming to him in this manner. On this particular occasion, Patrick was having difficulty deprogramming a member of a communal group. Eventually he told Streiker, "I've finally broken him! First I had to program him so that I could deprogram him. He didn't know he was in a cult."[21]

Even though this rationale is incredibly bizarre, some people are actually willing to accept it as valid. The reality is that these deprogramming victims were *never* "programmed" until they were placed in the hands of the anti-cult mental health "gurus" or the deprogrammers. Streiker suggests that Margaret Singer engages in a similar practice. He states that from personally observing Singer interview her clients, "Singer tells them what their experience was: She provides an interpretation or frame of reference for them to understand their own experience in a manner that is antagonistic to the particular group to which they have been converted. It could be said that she programs them."[22]

Despite the absurdity of this practice of "programming" people into believing they were in a "cult," this is what actually appears to be happening. One of the reasons for this conclusion is that individuals who were members of such diverse groups as fundamentalist Christian groups, the Hare Krishna movement (a religious group with Hindu origins), the Church of Scientology (a group that studies the mind and spirit), TM (another group derived from Hinduism), The Way International (another Christian group) and the Unification Church, all come out of the deprogramming process saying remarkably similar things! Is this because the "cults" are so similar to each other (see discussion in Chapter 7) or because the faithbreakers are "programming" their victims to say exactly the same things?

What becomes clear is that those who have gone through this coercive, demeaning process are persuaded to make statements of terrible "cult" practices because of the intense physical and emotional pressure that is brought to bear on them.[23] This tremendous pressure leads to an emotional climax where the victim can no longer resist and ultimately "caves in" so that he or she can find relief.[24] The only way out of this spiritual, emotional and psychological torture is to accept the views of the faithbreaker. No alternative viewpoint is allowed, and it is usually at this time that statements of disavowal and denunciation are signed.

In some instances victims are able to feign this "deconversion," but more often they are unable to do so because they feel it would be tantamount to betraying their most precious beliefs. Thus, once they have been pressured into submission and statements of renunciation, there is little chance that their guilty conscience will allow them to return. Having been drawn into such a stance, some victims of this process have continued their active involvement in the anti-cult movement, serving as public spokesmen and offering the "smoking gun" quality of evidence that makes their stories persuasive to many unfamiliar with the genre. And it is these statements of renunciation that have inevitably been picked up by the media.

As suggested earlier, the experience of those who have undergone deprogramming is in stark contrast to those who left voluntarily. From his research Stuart Wright observes as follows:

> *Accounts by **voluntary** defectors are generally characterized by greater tolerance and flexibility in arriving at an understanding of one's previous involvement. Unlike their deprogrammed counterparts, these former members rarely claim that their participation in the group is a product of psychological manipulation. Only 9% of those interviewed chose to describe their participation and commitment in this way. Conversely, 91% of the sample felt their participation was entirely voluntary and specifically avoided the language and rhetoric of brainwashing. To my knowledge, all of the respondents were aware of the controversy, and many were quite critical of the term "brainwashing" altogether.*[25]

Psychiatrist Lee Coleman in his article "New Religions and 'Deprogramming': Who's Brainwashing Whom?" suggests that claims of brainwashing by former members of new religions should not be considered "neutral." Numerous studies have indicated that although many people freely leave new religious movements if they no longer desire to continue their involvement, Coleman writes, "it is only those subjected to forced de-indoctrination who speak of 'brainwashing' or 'mind-control'. Such persons have indeed succumbed to Lifton's 'mystical manipulation' at the hands of parents and their allies."[26]

Psychologist Trudy Solomon makes a similar observation in her study of 100 former Unification Church members. She quotes one respondent who complained: "I felt a compulsion from deprogrammers, family and friends to categorize the Moon experience as bad, negative, what have you, even if unconsciously. I resented this and it made it more difficult to find a balance."[27]

A study by James R. Lewis of the University of North Carolina at Chapel Hill, using 154 former members of new religious groups, arrives at the same conclusion. He states that "it is all too clear that former 'cultists' who affiliate with the anti-cult movement are encouraged to reinterpret their membership in the worst possible terms." Lewis adds that "it is only a small step from there to see how a former cult member might also be influenced to view her or his *post*-membership period in a negative light (as an example of what the 'cult' had 'done' to them)."[28]

His findings were so disturbing to some members of the anti-cult movement (Citizens Freedom Foundation (CFF) which has since changed its name to "Cult Awareness Network" (CAN)) that they sought to have him dismissed from his graduate program at Syracuse University and to have his research project halted. Lewis reports:

> *It appears to me that CFF—far from being concerned about 'questionable' research methods—knew that genuine data had been gathered, and feared the publication of such legitimate research. In the absence of a convincing criticism of the research itself, CFF was*

> *willing to employ an 'underhanded' attack on the character of the researcher. The fact that this tactic was utilized by the director of the largest anti-cult organization in North America indicates that this event was more than the result of a simple oversight on the part of one overzealous anti-cultist.*[29]

Brock Kilbourne and James T. Richardson have coined the term "cultphobia" to describe the "sometimes obsessive, irrational fear of the so-called cults." They suggest that members of the anti-cult movement have developed intense exaggerated fears that are entirely disproportionate to any threat from the new religions. "They resort to the obsessive telling of atrocity tales" and many redefine their lives around a "messianic mission" to fight against the spread of the cults.[30]

Reinterpretation of "Cult" Experience

One theme that has frequently recurred in reports about tales by ex-members is their need to reinterpret their past experiences, particularly in the context of the aftermath of a deprogramming experience. For these people, "admitting" they were once in a "cult" is almost like admitting "I had AIDS" or "I had herpes." It is not easy to say, "Oh, then I went to graduate school, then I was a 'Moonie' and then I got married." There is a powerful sense that they have to renounce it for fear of peer disapproval.

University of Nevada sociologist James T. Richardson agrees with this analysis. He describes the necessity for someone who has gone through the deprogramming or faithbreaking process to explain his or her time in "the cult." He says "it is in everyone's interest to excuse the person, and to blame the group of membership. The account thus negotiated serves as a handy device that all concerned can use to explain to interested parties what happened to the person during those 'missing years' of their life."[31]

This is particularly important for normalizing relationships with family, to remove the sense of guilt and to be accepted and loved.[32] It also serves as a very therapeutic way for society or the status quo to justify its lifestyle. The apostate or defector is always used in this manner to "make us look good and them look bad."[33]

The use of Lifton's Chapter 22 has been most prominent and effective for this purpose. The terminology such as "milieu control," "mystical manipulation," "demand for purity" and "cult of confession" serves to provide an alternate explanation to the adherent who has just gone through the intensity of a faithbreaking. For such an individual, there is tremendous need for a transitional mythology that explains everything to people. However, when examined closely, Lifton's terminology, like Singer's six parameters, are so broad and ambiguous that they can relate to almost anything. In fact, they relate far more closely to the faithbreaking experience than the new religious movements. Nevertheless, for the newly created apostate, they serve a very useful purpose.

New religions experts Thomas Robbins and Dick Anthony make a similar point in an article entitled "'Cults' vs. 'Shrinks': Psychiatry and the Control of Religious Movements." They suggest that the retrospective accounts of ex-members of any religious group necessarily reflect the shifting attitudes, needs and interests of the individual in his or her present situation. They cite Peter Berger who explains that people continually reconstruct their past experiences to adjust them to their present orientations.[34] Robbins and Anthony add:

> *A convert to a religious sect may, without intending to deceive, exaggerate the depths of depravity and disorientation to which he or she had sunk prior to being 'saved.' Similarly, a disillusioned ex-sectarian may exaggerate the degree to which he or she was 'brainwashed,' regimented or involved in spectacularly bizarre and depraved scenes prior to being 'saved' by deprogramming. Such reinterpretations may be reinforced by various significant others such as parents,therapists or deprogrammer; moveover, 'brainwashing' conceptualizations of past sectarian experiences may be highly functional and psychologically rewarding.*[35]

Dean Kelley offers a similar comment: "After a person has doubly defected—once from parental values and then from the religious group—strong pressures for self-justification and the expiation of guilt are set in motion. These often take the form of insisting, 'I was fooled, I was victimized.'"[36]

British sociologist James Beckford discovered from his extensive research that parents of former members often go to great lengths to absolve themselves of any responsibility for their offspring's involvement in the "cult." Wishing to interpret their offspring's participation as "brainwashing," they often badger them to give negative details of their experience, but in the majority of cases without success. "While overall the experience had not worked for them, they still recalled good times and positive aspects."[37]

In his 1978 *Fordham Law Review* article John Le Moult attempts to analyze what happens psychologically to a person after he renounces his former beliefs.[38] The problem for a person who has had his faith broken through a deprogramming experience is that although the anti-cultists imposed a new identity on him—one that is acceptable to his parents—his own identity may still be linked to his former beliefs. Thus, he has to choose between two sets of beliefs—either to return to the group or accept the beliefs that his parents desire. Often the difficulty is that once a person has renounced his former beliefs, he has a tremendous sense of guilt and a fear of being judged by his former religious associates as having betrayed them. This fear of returning is, of course, powerfully reinforced by his family and the faithbreakers. They tell him such things as "they will never associate with you again—they hate you..."

As Le Moult points out, it is essential for one's sense of identity to make this choice: "It is necessary for integration of the personality. Identity is vital to the sense of self that each person must have and it must be supported by overt action." Le Moult adds that the "deprogrammed youth may feel a powerful need to attack his former religion, not because it is evil, but because he cannot live with his new identity unless he does."[39]

A useful summary of the "apostate phenomenon" is given by Bromley and Shupe in their book *Strange Gods:*

The similarities in horror stories told by apostate or ex-members of new religions are not the result of their all having experienced the same brainwashing processes...Many anti-cultists claim that brainwashing and mind control must be real processes because so many deprogrammed ex-members repeat the same accusations and stories.

This is specious logic, however. We argue that the family situation puts pressures on ex-members to reinterpret their cult experiences in the same self-serving way, and that after deprogramming became a more widespread practice, a folk-lore of deprogramming developed. Deprogrammers themselves implanted interpretations in the midst of new religions' members. Deprogrammers are like the American colonials who persecuted 'witches': a confession, drawn up before the suspect was brought in for torturing, on the judges' fantasies about witchcraft, was signed under duress and then treated as justification for the torture.

In the end, the similarity of ex-members' stories is not the result of similar experiences but rather of artificial and imposed reinterpretations by persons serving their own needs and purposes.[40]

There is no question that the ex-member stories played a key role in arousing public hostility against the Unification Church during the 1970s. Their impact, however, has been diminishing in recent years as studies by such scholars as James T. Richardson, David Bromley, Anson Shupe, Joseph Fichter, Herbert Richardson, James Lewis, Trudy Solomon, Stuart Wright and many others have come to light. Unfortunately, scholarly publications often do not reach the general public's attention. There are two main reasons for this: the public is much more attracted to the horrific tales of apostate members than it is to scholarly, scientific research papers and secondly, the media have likewise found the apostate tales to be much more sensational and therefore profitable.

References

1. Movies such as "Ticket to Heaven," "Moonchild" and "Split Images" play on the sensational cult hysteria. See Leo Pfeffer in Herbert Richardson (ed.), *Constitutional Issues in the Case of Rev. Moon* (New York: Edwin Mellen, 1984) 536. Lowell Streiker suggested that such movies are part of a propaganda process which asserts that anything which is not traditional is bad for you. Thus, the so-called "cults" are depicted as not good for you. Streiker interview with author, Aug. 14, 1986.

2. See James Beckford, "'Brainwashing' and 'Deprogramming' in Britain: The Social Sources of Anti-Cult Sentiment," in David G. Bromley and James T. Richardson (eds.), *The Brainwashing/Deprogramming Controversy: Sociological, Psychological, Legal, and Historical Perspectives* (New Brunswick, N.J.: Transaction Books, 1983.

3. Stuart A. Wright, "Post-Involvement Attitudes of Voluntary Defectors From Controversial New Religious Movements," *Journal for the Scientific Study of Religion,* Vol. 23 (2): 172-182.

4. David Bromley, "Ted Patrick," supra, 2.

5. Trudy Solomon, "Integrating the 'Moonie' Experience: A Survey of Ex-Members of the Unification Church," in T. Robbins and D.Anthony (eds.), *In Gods We Trust,* (New Brunswick, NJ: Transaction, 1981).

6. Wright, supra, 3.

7. Mose Durst, *To Bigotry, No Sanction* (Chicago: Regnery Gateway, 1984) 155.

8. It should be stated clearly that members of the Unification Church often do work for long hours with little sleep. This is based on a belief that this is an extremely urgent time according to God's providential timetable. Yet this is not unique to the Unification Church. Many other

religious figures have exhorted their followers with similar urgency—which is not to mention the intense lifestyles of many lawyers, business people and artists who frequently work under similar conditions.

9. Bromley and Shupe assert that the stereotypical image of new religions bears "little resemblance to reality." David G. Bromley and Anson D. Shupe, Jr., "The Archetypal Cult: Conflict and the Social Construction of Deviance," in Gene J. James (ed.), *The Family and The Unification Church* (New York: Rose of Sharon, 1983) 20.

10. Fichter, supra, 12.

11. Herbert Richardson, supra, xxviii.

12*. Ibid. This compares to the many horrific stories told by ex-priest William Hogan in *Popery! As It Was and as It Is: Also, Auricular Confessions: and Popish Nunneries* (Hartford, 1855). See also David Brion Davis, "Some Themes of Counter-Subversion: An Analysis of Anti-Masonic, Anti-Catholic, and Anti-Mormon Literature," *The Mississippi Valley Historical Review,* Vol. XLVII, No.2, Sept. 1960, 205.

12. Herbert Richardson, ibid. Apostate Mormons, such as Ann Eliza Young, traveled similar lecture circuits in the 1870's.

13. Ibid.

14. Joseph Fichter, "Hammering the Heretics," in *Witness,* Vol. 66, No. 1, Jan. 1983, 5.

15. Maria Ward, *Female Life Among the Mormons* (New York: J.C. Derby, 1855) 12. A frequent accusation against Mormons was that they "mesmerized" people in order "to delude, and even seduce, unwitting victims." They were also accused of using "animal magnetism" and "hypnosis." See Gary L. Bunker and Davis Bitton, "Mesmerism and Mormonism," *BYU Studies,* Vol. 15, No. 2, 146.

16. D. Bromley and A. Shupe, *Strange Gods* (Boston: Beacon Press, 1981) 200-201. James T. Richardson agreed. See "Leaving and Labeling: Voluntary and Coerced Disaffiliation From Religious Social Movements," 16. Forthcoming in Kurt Lang (ed.), *Research in Social Movements, Conflicts and Change,* Vol. 9. (Greenwich, CT: JAI Press, 1985).

17. Affidavit of James Anthony Beatrice, May 14, 1981. (Author's files).

18. Affidavit of Marta Cortes, Sept. 9, 1982. (Author's files).

19. Affidavit of Laura Jean Wilson, Sept. 18, 1978. (Author's files).

20. Interview with author, July 29, 1986.

21. See Lowell Streiker, *Mind-Bending,* supra, 37.

22. Streiker interview, supra. One such person who was interviewed by Singer, John Hovard, confirmed this. Hovard, who was one of the five Unification Church members placed under conservatorship in the *Katz v. Superior Court* case (see Chapter 8) stated that Singer manipulated the interview to get him to say what she wanted to hear. He felt certain that she had already made up her mind about his mental state before the interview began, by virtue of his membership in the Unification Church. Interview with author, July 30, 1986. A further confirmation of this practice came from Judge Stuart Pollak in *Molko & Leal v. HSA* as quoted earlier in Chapter 2.

23. This is not to say that every person has the same experience. Some apostates who go through the deprogramming experience feel that they are genuine in their opposition to their former faith.

24. John Le Moult offered several useful insights in "Deprogramming Members of Religious Sects," supra, 606-608. In particular, he compared this emotional breakdown and caving in to intense pressure to the break

described by Joost A.M. Meerloo as having been suffered by victims of Nazi interrogation. Meerloo wrote: "Several victims of the Nazi inquistion have told me that the moment of surrender occurred suddenly and against their will. For days they had faced the fury of their interrogators, and then suddenly they fell apart. 'All right, all right, you can have anything you want.' And then came hours of remorse, of resolution, of a desperate wish to return to their previous position of firm resistance. They wanted to cry out: 'Don't ask me anything else. I won't answer.' And yet something in them, that conforming, complying being hidden in all of us, was on the move. This sudden surrender often happened after an unexpected accusation, a shock, a humiliation that particularly hurt, a punishment that burned, a surprising logic in the inquisitor's question that could not be counterargued." Joost A.M. Meerloo, *The Rape of the Mind: The Psychology of Thought Control, Menticide, and Brainwashing* (Cleveland: World, 1956).

25. Wright, supra, 14. See also David A. Snow and Richard Machalek, "The Sociology of Conversion," *Annual Review of Sociology (1984), 179-180.*

26. See Thomas Robbins, William C. Shepherd and James McBride (eds.), *Cults, Culture and The Law* (Chico, CA: Scholars Press, 1985) 73.

27. Trudy Soloman, supra, 288.

28. James R. Lewis, "Information Disease and the Legitimization of Religious Repression," presented to the annual meeting of the Association for the Sociology of Religion, August 25-27, 1984. This paper, after some redrafting, was later published as a Research Note entitled "Reconstructing the 'Cult' Experience" in *Sociological Analysis,* Vol. 47 (2), 1986, 151.

29. (Unpublished, retained in author's files).

30. Brock K. Kilbourne and James T. Richardson, "Cultphobia," *Thought, Fordham University Quarterly,* Vol. LXI, June, 1986, 260-62.

31. James T. Richardson, "Leaving and Labeling," supra, 17.

32. Streiker interview, August 13, 1986.

33. Ibid.

34. Thomas Robbins and Dick Anthony, "'Cults' vs. 'Shrinks': Psychiatry and the Control of Religious Movements" in Herbert Richardson (ed.), *New Religions and Mental Health,* supra, 51-52; citing Peter Berger, *Invitation to Sociology* (New York: Anchor, 1963) 57. Chris Elkins, who is a former Unification Church member, makes a similar point: "Too often an ex-cult member mixes into his experience strong doses of vengeance and hate. Often, his former colleagues are right when they accuse him of distorting the truth." Elkins, supra, 9.

35. Robbins and Anthony, ibid., 52.

36. Kelley, supra, 31.

37. Beckford, supra. See also Bromley and Shupe, *Strange Gods,* supra, 201. In an earlier study of ex-Unification Church members, Beckford observed: "...when I have questioned ex-members more closely about the way they felt toward their former colleagues 'during membership,' their answers have generally indicated that they felt nothing but love and admiration for them." James Beckford, "Through the Looking-Glass and Out the Other Side: Withdrawal from Reverend Moon's Unification Church," *Archives des Sciences Sociales des Religion,* Vol. 45, 1978, 109.

38. Le Moult, supra, 608, n. 67.

39. Ibid.

40. Bromley and Shupe, *Strange Gods,* supra, 203-204.

Chapter 6

THE CONVERSION EXPERIENCE: PARALLELS WITH TRADITIONAL RELIGIONS

The History of Conversion

The attack on new religious movements is by implication a subtle attack on the very act of conversion to any religious faith. The fundamental argument of the anti-cult psychologists and psychiatrists is not that religious adherents are a threat to themselves or to others, but that *religious faith is itself an involuntary, mentally coerced act.* In their view, a free person would never voluntarily convert to or adhere to a religion, particularly one with any kind of intensity. Thus, it is the act of converting to or affiliating with a religion that is prima facie evidence of mental illness and a loss of free choice.[1]

There are also those of strong religious conviction who attack Unification Church conversions as being inauthentic on theological grounds. Some religiously motivated critics claim that Unification Church members are under "mind control" simply because they have lost their own adherents to the Unification Church fold or because they do not understand or accept Unification theology. There are even some, such as Jewish anti-conversionists, who believe that conversion should not be allowed at all. This is because they believe that being a Jew is a matter of inheritance rather than choice. Therefore, they do not actively evangelize, nor do they take kindly to any other religion evangelizing members of the Jewish faith. In fact, the nation of Israel has passed anti-conversion laws.[2] The end result is that some segments of the Jewish population have been among the strongest proponents of the brainwashing/mind control theory simply because any form of conversion to any religious faith is seen as a threat to the Jewish people.[3] What they do not seem to realize is that by making such unfair attacks on the religious beliefs and practices of other religious groups, they are ultimately placing religious freedom in jeopardy for all.

To evaluate these views, a clearer understanding of religious conversion is needed. Are the "anti-cult" psychologists and psychiatrists correct when they say that joining a religious group such as the Unification Church cannot be compared to conversion to mainline religious denominations? According to sociologists Brock Kilbourne and James T. Richardson, empirical studies "indicate a remarkable similarity between conversion to deviant or minority religions and those to more established, traditional religions."[4] Thus, there are some very clear parallels that can be drawn. The following examples demonstrate that hostility to the conversion experience is nothing new.

On the road to Damascus, Saul of Tarsus, a persecutor of the followers of Jesus of Nazareth, was converted. The conversion experience of St. Paul is the classic example of what sudden and total Christian conversion is about.[5] What did the great Roman philosophers and writers think of the early Christians and their "conversion" experience?

> "There is a group hated for their abominations called 'Christian.'" (Tacitus)
>
> "The Christians are a class of men given to a new and wicked superstition." (Suetonius)
>
> "They are like frogs holding a symposium around a swamp." (Celsius)[6]

The radical conversion experience has always opened individuals to a new view of self, of society and of God. The consequences of conversion have been significant, not only for the individual, but also for the reaction from others—a reaction often based on ignorance. The very beginning of Judeo-Christian culture provides the archetypal model of conversion and the anti-conversion response. In reading the description of Abraham receiving God's call in scriptures, one may imagine that Abraham's father could not understand why Abraham chose to abandon his lucrative idol-making business to worship an ethical, monotheistic, living, yet invisible God.[7]

Thus, it is also understandable that Haskell Lazere, representing both the American Jewish Committee and the American Jewish Congress of New York, wrote in opposition to proposed legislation in New York State which would have opened conversion to any religion to examination by the State:

> *Under the standards adopted by these bills, the transformation of Moses upon seeing the burning bush would have been grounds for the appointment of a temporary guardian by a court, since that experience was not a "gradual change" resulting from "maturation or education."*[8]

Radical Changes

In the conversion experience everything seems to take on new meaning. It is a moment of new possibilities, and it is therefore one of the most vital of human experiences because within it lies the limitless possibilities of human creativity and "divinity." William James, in his well-known book *The Varieties of Religious Experience,* makes the same point when he writes about conversion as a moment that awakens a person to the possibility of fulfilling his internal urging towards a fuller or deeper meaning in life. It is a desire which had previously lain below the surface of life's daily activities but which suddenly takes the central place in his life.[9]

In his book *Psychology of Religion* Paul E. Johnson explains that although there are many different ways to experience conversion, a genuine conversion is frequently the outcome of a crisis which takes *all* of a person and directs his whole life upon a new course.[10] He described "a sense of desperate conflict in which one is so involved that his whole meaning and destiny are at stake in a life-or-death, all-or-none significance." Johnson adds that if, at this moment, the person reaches out to God, willing to give all of himself, then he may be radically changed in a true religious conversion.[11] It is important, however, to capture this moment. He suggests that religion cannot afford to forget this sense of urgency in nurturing new birth. That is the value of the revival meeting which "puts the crisis now, in this very hour, with eloquent contrast between the way of life and the way of death."[12]

The great evangelist and founder of Methodism, John Wesley, eloquently described the process for his converts as being born again, born of the spirit where "We are inwardly renewed by the power of God." Wesley said that God instills a powerful love into our hearts through the Holy Ghost (or Holy Spirit) which produces a feeling of love for all of mankind as the children of God. At the same time, it expels "the love of the world, the love of pleasure, of ease, of honor, of money, together with pride, anger, self-will and every other evil temper; in a word, changing the 'earthly, sensual, devilish mind' into 'the mind which was in Christ Jesus.'"[13]

Conversion is often a moment when the convert decides to make radical changes in his lifestyle, to totally dedicate his life to God. This is crucial, since even the most profound conversion experience can quickly fade if it is not acted upon. Christian clergymen frequently urge their congregations to make the conversion experience real in their lives by making significant changes in their lifestyles. In a recent sermon, a minister of the African Methodist Episcopal Church expressed concern that all too many Christians just go through the "motions" of conversion or rebirth, but without really changing their lives. He exhorted his congregation to have a genuine rebirth experience so that they could truly say: "I have been transformed; I have changed; my life is *different.*" He added that if our family and friends are not able to see dramatic changes in our lives, then we have not truly been converted.[14]

There is nothing new or sinister in the dramatic changes experienced by converted youth, adds John Le Moult in his frequently cited *Fordham Law Review* article "Deprogramming Members of Religious Sects."[15] The fact that these dramatic changes frequently involve an intense and "totalistic" dedication to a religious faith is quite typical. The demands that Jesus Christ made upon those who would be his disciples were very heavy indeed and required an intense faith. As Jesus said to one man who had asserted that he was obedient to all of God's Ten Commandments: "One thing you still lack. Sell all that you have and distribute to the poor, and you will have treasure in heaven; and come, follow me."[16]

The prominent theologian Paul Tillich was quoted in the landmark United States Supreme Court decision *United States v. Seeger* as saying that to speak of God is to "speak of the depths of your life, of the source of your being, of your ultimate concern, of what you take seriously without any reservation."[17] In another leading Supreme Court decision, *Welsh v. United States,* Justice John Harlan distinguished religion from "mere adherence to ethical or moral beliefs in general," and argued for identifying religion by the "intensity of moral conviction with which a belief is held."[18] Legal commentator Robert N. Shapiro writes that the "hallmark of religion" is "the willingness to stake one's all on the belief system one adopts. The person must have conviction; he must have a faith that binds him to an ultimate concern."[19]

Religious belief provides a means of dealing with the world in a way that makes sense. Tillich expressed this point in a poignant way;

> *If the foundations of the place and all places begin to crumble...only two alternatives remain—despair, which is the certainty of eternal destruction, or faith, which is the certainty of eternal salvation. 'The world itself shall crumble, but...my salvation knows no end,' says the Lord...This is what we should call religion, or more precisely, the religious ground for all religion.*[20]

It is this kind of belief that leads a believer to offer his life to God, to submit himself to the guidance and direction of his spiritual elders. This, however, is another point of contention for anti-religionists. The concept of submitting oneself to religious authority or church hierarchy is considered unequivocal evidence of mind control.

Yet, as Shapiro points out, it is normally quite legitimate in our society for one to "consciously submit to an authoritarian system that prescribes appropriate thoughts as well as actions." Shapiro adds that "established religions commonly prescribe authoritarian standards of behavior. Two examples are the Roman Catholic Catechism or the Talmudic rules."[21] Furthermore, the concept of submission lies at the very basis of the Christian faith. Jesus made the supreme sacrifice after he said the words, "Not my will, (Lord), but thine."[22]

One basis for the allegations of mental illness or mind control in the non-approved religions is that their beliefs are not rational, but rather are based upon myths and "mystical manipulation." Anti-religious psychologists and psychiatrists have utilized Lifton's description of such manipulation:

> *The individual responds to the manipulations through developing what I call the psychology of the pawn. Feeling himself unable to escape from forces more powerful than himself, he subordinates everything to adapting himself to them. He becomes sensitive to all kinds of cues, expert at anticipating environmental pressures, and skillful in riding them in such a way that his psychological energies merge with the tide rather than turn painfully against himself. This requires that he participate actively in the manipulation of others, as well as in the endless rounds of betrayals and self betrayals which are required.*[23]

This could easily be interpreted as an attack on all religion. In his excellent article, "Of Robots, Persons and the Protection of Religious Beliefs," Shapiro points out that even the so-called "established" religions have many tenets that may be considered manipulative or bizarre by any rational standard. He cites, by way of example, the cases which have tested whether creationists' belief in the literal truth of Genesis qualifies as science. He writes "no one has seriously suggested that in addition to barring 'creation science' from public school curricula, the creationists should also be deemed mentally ill because of their fundamentalist tenets." Shapiro adds that in a similar way, "Jesus' rising from the dead or God's speaking to Moses from a burning bush are articles of faith to some, yet skeptics' opinions that such beliefs are absurd does not allow them to have the believers committed as mentally ill."[24]

Another criticism of the new religions is that members lose their sense of identity, that a group identity develops, with a specific focus on a "charismatic leader." Lifton describes a tendency to "all-or-nothing emotional alignment [which] exists within everyone" and which can be exploited by "those ideologies which are most sweeping in content and most ambitious—or Messianic—in their claims, whether religious, political, or scientific. And where totalitarianism exists, a religion, or political movement, or even a scientific organization becomes little more than an exclusive cult."[25]

The problem with this kind of analysis is that it can easily be applied against *any* religion or *any* group with which a psychiatrist happens to disagree. The powerful, fervent and intense devotion that many Christians, especially the Pentecostals, offer to Jesus Christ would clearly seem to cause one to lose his or her identity or sense of self. Yet this is precisely what Christianity seeks to do. The followers of Jesus or St. Francis or John Wesley or George Fox or Joseph Smith or Billy Graham would all qualify for Lifton's "looney bin!" At the very least, they would certainly require deprogramming!

There is much more that could be said about the intensity and totalism of the practices of more established churches which the "anti-cult" network would never *openly* challenge. The Church of the Middle Ages, which is the parent of all of Christianity today, had some very intense and "totalistic" practices. The Roman Catholic monk Thomas à Kempis in his famous book *Imitation of Christ* documented the monastic lifestyle:

> *It is the transformation of one's way of life and the complete mortification of the passions that make a true religion. He who seeks in this life anything but God alone and the salvation of his soul will find nothing but trouble and grief...No one can remain here unless he is ready to humble himself with all his heart for love of God.*[26]

This would certainly seem to qualify as a "totalistic" lifestyle in Lifton's terms, not to mention "guilt manipulation" and "submission." But there is more:

> *How countless and constant were the trials endured by the Apostles, Martyrs, Confessors, Virgins, and all those others who strove to follow in the footsteps of Christ. These all hated their lives in this world, that they might keep them to life eternal....*
>
> *All day long they labored, and the night they gave to continuous prayer; even as they worked, they never ceased from mental prayer. They spent all their time with profit, every hour seeming short in the service of God. They often forgot even their bodily needs in the great sweetness of contemplation. They renounced all riches, dignities, honors, friends and kindred; they desired*

> *to possess nothing in this world. Scarcely would they take the necessities of life, and only with reluctance would they provide for the needs of the body....*
> *To themselves they were nothing, but in the eyes of God they were precious and beloved. Grounded in true humility, they lived in simple obedience, they walked in charity and patience; and thus daily increased in the spirit, and received great grace from God.*[27]

This tradition has carried on through this century. The Dominican Order of the Roman Catholic Church stresses rote exercises, requiring daily repetitive recitations of "the ancient Office of the Pater Noster...for Matins, twenty-eight Paters and Aves, for Vespers fourteen, and seven for each of the little Hours."[28] One theologian recently noted that "Anyone who has read Thomas Merton's *Seven Story Mountain* can discover that he [as a Trappist monk] went through 'sleep deprivation' (called vigils by the monks), 'food withdrawal' (called fasting), 'monotonous chanting,' (called choir), 'loss of facial hair' (called tonsure), 'manipulation of the environment' and 'control over information and channels of communication' (called cloister and rules of silence)."[29]

Conversion Experience for Unification Church Members

Unificationists follow in this great religious tradition, although with considerably less intensity than the Dominicans or the Trappists. Catholic sociologist Joseph Fichter wrote approvingly of the faith of the hundreds of Unification Church members he has encountered: "These young people are asserting that religion is precisely what it is defined to be: a probing relationship in search of truth, transcendence, and the sacred. To commune with the Infinite, to be in the presence of God—here we are talking about the essence of religion."[30]

Unificationists would describe their conversion in ways quite similar to what has been quoted above. Life is essentially a period of growth from birth to passing in which we journey on the road to finding God and ultimately becoming one in heart and mind with Him. For most members, their initial contact with the Unification Church marks a rather dramatic event whereby they are confronted and challenged by the need to travel this road with greater seriousness and urgency. They are made aware of just how far they really are from the goal of achieving Godliness, but are given fresh perspective and a clearer road map with which to hasten this journey. There is a profound belief that Jesus meant what he said when he urged: "You, therefore, must be perfect as your Heavenly Father is perfect."[31]

The Unification view of conversion may be compared to the view of another prominent theologian of this century, Reinhold Niebuhr, who described the need for the conversion experience to overcome the preoccupation with self or the self-centeredness that is so prevalent in this world. He wrote:

> *The self in this state of preoccupation with itself must be 'broken' and 'shattered' or, in the Pauline phrase, 'crucified.' It cannot be saved merely by being enlightened. It is a unity and therefore cannot be drawn out of itself merely by extending its perspective upon interests beyond itself. If it remains self-centered, it merely uses its wider perspective to bring more lives and interests under the dominion of its will-to-power. The necessity of its being shattered at the very center of its being gives perennial validity to the strategy of evangelistic sects, which seek to induce the crisis of conversion.*[32]

Yet this threshold experience of Unification Church members is often not their first religious or conversion experience, since most have had a long history of reaching out to God or to some sort of ideal or dream. Nor is it the final experience of conversion or upheaval, since life is a continual journey or process of maturing in faith and love for God and fellow man.

John Wesley stressed the tremendous importance of this constant renewal[33] as does Paul Johnson, who writes that "conversion is an incident in the process of religious growth." He admonishes that "without continuous growth before and after the climax, conversion is unreal and futile."[34]

In a similar vein, Roman Catholic Thomas McGowan explains his view that conversion is a "spiritual journey towards self-realization in God." He adds:

> *Conversion, as Niebuhr ably observed, is a never-ending process and occurs every time the self is confronted with the claims of God and so is moved off center. A person develops by becoming a new self that transcends the previous self. Conversion then is the marker event which announces the successful completion of the journey through a crisis to a higher spiritual life; even more fundamentally, it is the whole process of growth in the work of self-transcendence.*[35]

Another Catholic theologian, Richard De Maria, Vice President for Academic Affairs at Iona College, confronts the issue of the suddenness of conversion for many members of the Unification Church in an article called "A Psycho-Social Analysis of Religious Conversion." He traces the long history of sudden conversion experiences which, for some, is the *normal,* preferable way to salvation. He quotes John Wesley as saying that conversion or "sanctification is commonly, if not always, an instantaneous work."[36] This leads De Maria to conclude as follows:

> *Conversion, then, can be viewed as a method of re-education whereby one seeks to "undo" the unbalanced or unhealthy programming with which he or she has grown up. The sudden conversion seems to be the only way in which some people can enter into that broadening of consciousness which is the prerequisite of growth (which others accomplish gradually under the influence of more gentle proddings.) The list of men and women whose lives of holiness and service have followed upon sudden and radical reversal is extensive—extensive enough to warrant a benevolent view of the process. My point, in summary, is that sudden conversion does seem to be a valid path in and toward spiritual growth. The suddenness of the conversion of many Unification Church members should not be used as a criterion of inauthenticity. If one wants to consider sudden conversion as an unauthentic form of religious experience, he should at least realize that he does this in the face of a long tradition of acceptance.*[37]

Despite the common perception that most Unification Church members joined as a result of a "sudden" conversion experience at some secluded location, the research of Thomas McGowan points to a somewhat different conclusion. Based on a survey of 74 Unification Church members, McGowan concludes that the conversion experiences of these respondents jibes quite well with the conclusions of noted psychiatrists Jean Piaget and Erik Erikson concerning the developmental processes at work. He notes that very few indicated any kind of impetuous conversion: most spoke of months or years characterized by feelings of incompleteness and searching. "For most, deliverance came gradually, and the conversion experience marked an intellectual breakthrough with the discovery of truth in the Divine Principle (the theology of the Unification Church) or an emotional catharsis with the discovery of love, acceptance, and friendship in the new community." He adds that their conversion experience produced the feelings of peace, new energy, and sense of achievement that are associated with Abraham Maslow's description of the "peak-experience."[38]

De Maria also confronts the allegation of "manipulative" dynamics such as secluded retreat centers where people are subjected to a rigid and exhausting schedule of "mind-numbing theology" in "an atmosphere of communal love and acceptance." Without accepting that these allegations are factual, De Maria recalls that those responsible for spiritual growth have long recognized that "the dawning of new consciousness is difficult because it requires the partial breakdown of the former consciousness." Over the years, spiritual teachers have developed methods which help bring about this process for those who have difficulty. He describes it as a "death/life process wherein the old consciousness is broken to make room for the new."[39]

During the 1950's, Trappist monk Thomas Merton wrote that spiritual life requires discipline—a discipline that must "have a certain element of severity about it. Otherwise it will never set us free from the passions." He stressed that it is necessary to be strict with ourselves. "If we do not command ourselves severely to pray and do penance at certain definite times, and make up our mind to keep our resolutions in spite of notable inconvenience and difficulty, we will quickly be deluded by our own excuses and let ourselves be led away by weakness and caprice."[40]

The intensity of a Unification religious retreat sounds tame in comparison to the powerful revivalist movement which formed the backbone of American religion during the eighteenth and nineteenth centuries. De Maria describes in vivid detail the circuit-riding preachers who traveled the country during these years searching after and finding those who were "willing to submit themselves to the total emotional onslaught of the revival experience." People came from miles around to camp for several days in spots cleared in forests where they would socialize, engage in "hours of exhausting singing, praying, and witnessing, and submitted to the impassioned and terrifying sermons of 'hell fire' preachers. And they did this in the hope that, immersed in this believing experience, they would find that vision which they believed to be essential to salvation, but which many could not discover without charismatic help."[41]

As De Maria also points out, many contemporary therapy groups seek to bring their followers to new awareness through even more dramatic methods. He cites, by way of example, the group-encounter movement where participants willingly commit themselves to such practices as "sleepless 'marathon' sessions of probing, insult, nudity, attack, and cajoling in the hope that the experience will free them from emotional blocks and lead them to some new consciousness."[42] Gordon Melton and Robert Moore add that "[a] young Marine recruit undergoes ritual humiliation that dwarfs anything any religious group can muster."[43]

Another related issue addressed by De Maria and others is whether or not there is any physical coercion involved in the conversion process in the Unification Church. Some writers have asserted that if this had ever taken place, opponents of the Church could have successfully pressed criminal charges, an event that has not occurred. De Maria compares these allegations against the Unification Church to those made during periods of rabid anti-Catholic sentiment such as the mid-19th century when "the family and friends of a Rebecca Newell stormed St. Xavier's Convent in Providence, Rhode Island, in order to remove her by force, so sure were they that she was being kept there against her will."[44] De Maria's own research shows that there is no indication that such coercion exists in the Unification Church. He notes that many free-lance writers and reporters have attended Unification Church retreats (often surreptitiously) and have never reported physical coercion. He adds: "At present the only unquestionable physical coercion regarding the Church is that being practiced by the professional kidnappers and deprogrammers working on behalf of the parents."[45]

In what has been called the most thorough investigation ever made by an outsider into who becomes a Unification Church member, Eileen Barker, Dean of Undergraduate Studies at the London School of Economics and Political Science, came to the same conclusion in her book *The Making of a Moonie.* After more than five years of quantitative research of those who attended Unification Church workshops, she "found no evidence to suggest that physical coercion (in the forms of 'bodily constraint;' 'brain control' or 'biological suggestibility') was responsible for a person becoming a Moonie."[46] Based on another extensive study of Unification Church members, Trudy Solomon agrees: "Force and captivity are simply not conditions that apply to Moon's recruits."[47]

One of the major reasons that critics have made charges of such coercion is because of allegations that members of the Church are forced to break contact with their families. De Maria points out that it is conceivable that any member of any organization may be inclined to limit communication if he is constantly cajoled, berated or ridiculed for his involvement.[48] De Maria rhetorically asks: "What marriage counselor would not advise a young man or woman whose parents consistently berate or humiliate his new wife or her new husband to limit these contacts, because one's first duty is to his or her new life, new partner, and new vocation?" He adds that:

> *For centuries, the religious orders of the Christian Church have acted in much the same way: efforts are made to help family and friends to accept and support the decision of the member involved to embrace the communal vocation. But if parents' letters consist of little more than pleas to the son or daughter to return home, if the visits amount to little more than attacks by the family upon the theology, lifestyle, or mission of the novice, leaving him shaken and torn with grief, there is not a*

> *novice master or mistress who would not discourage any further communication, unless the family changes its posture.*[49]

The youthfulness of converts to the Unification Church has often been a point of contention as well. Detractors argue that the Church targets young people who are "emotionally impressionable and vulnerable."[50] However, the reality of conversion to any religious faith is that it frequently entails precisely these elements. Paul Johnson cites five studies made by psychologists that indicated the average age of conversion ranged between 12.7 and 16.6 years of age.[51] (In the Unification Church, the average age of conversion is the early 20s.)[52] Johnson suggests that "The later the conversion comes, the more intense and revolutionary it is, for the changes are more drastic and difficult."[53]

As for the vulnerability of converts, one study cited by Johnson reports that the most common preconversion experiences begin with "depression and pensive sadness." Other experiences include "restless anxiety and uncertainty, sense of sin, loss of sleep or appetite, feeling of estrangement from God, desire for a better life, doubt and questioning, earnest seriousness, weeping and nervousness."[54] Thus, it can be acknowledged that conversion frequently occurs during times of seriousness and searching, as well as times of transition. The Unification Church should not be subject to accusation on this account any more than any other religion.

The Current Threat

What becomes clear from a study of the religious phenomenon called conversion is that it has always been controversial. Dean Kelley, the prominent church-and-state expert of the National Council of Churches, writes that the allegations of bizarre behavior against the "so-called cult religious movements" are nothing new in the context of church history, or indeed of human history.[55]

Beyond this understanding of history, it is useful to be reminded that the Constitution of the United States as well as the United Nations Charter and the Universal Declaration of

Human Rights explicitly guarantee the right of free exercise of religion to each individual. As stated in Article 18 of the Universal Declaration of Human Rights:

> *Everyone has the right to freedom of thought, conscience and religion; the right includes* ***freedom to change his religion or belief,*** (emphasis added) *and freedom, either alone or in community with others and in public or private, to manifest his religion or belief in teaching, practice, worship and observance."*[56]

Thus, it should go without saying that this is a right that should exist without the interference of vigilante groups or the state. The well-known and highly-regarded church-and-state expert Leo Pfeffer warns us that:

> *The purpose of the first amendment's guarantee of freedom of religion was and is the protection of unpopular creeds and faiths. It needs no constitution to assure security for the Episcopalians, Methodists, Presbyterians, or other well-established and long-accepted religions. The heart of the first amendment would be mortally wounded if the religions we now call cults were excluded from the zone of its protection because of their disfavor in the eyes of government officials or of the majority of Americans*[57]

Of particular concern to those in the religious community is that the attacks of recent years are a growing sign of the "ever increasing secularization of a society that seeks to medicalize all human life and see everything therapeutically."[58] They are particularly appealing to parents who are unable to understand their offspring's rejection to society's secular career goals and their intense religious commitment. Thus, they "readily adopt the medical model which is represented by the brainwashing interpretation."[59]

Many people are concerned that the attacks by the mental health profession upon the intensity or depth of *any* religious faith pose a challenge and a threat to religious freedom for *all* faiths. There is a growing anxiety that religion is being slowly, subtly, yet steadily, removed from the "public square." It is no longer appropriate to pray, study or talk about God, let alone seek converts, in almost any public forum. And religion is all right, just so long as it is not taken too seriously, practiced too intensively or evangelized too strenuously. Rather than decreased protection, the more intense religious beliefs ought to bring *greater* protection.[60] As Shapiro cogently states:

> *Adherents who subject their reason to the demands of faith, and demonstrate the depth of their commitment by insisting upon their beliefs as ultimate concerns, should not find the intensity of their faith being used as proof of their incompetence. Otherwise, the fact of adherence to a particular faith could itself become evidence of mind control, and the only way to show control over one 's mind would be to renounce one's religion.*[61]

References

1. See Herbert Richardson (ed.), *New Religions and Mental Health,* supra xv.

2. Ibid., xx-xxi. Several Moslem nations have passed anti-conversion laws as well.

3. For full discussion, see Henry O. Thompson "A Study in Antisemitism" in Henry O. Thompson (ed.), *Unity in Diversity* (New York: Rose of Sharon Press, 1984).

4. Brock K. Kilbourne and James T. Richardson, "Anti-Religious Bias in DSM-III," supra, 27-28.

5. Acts, 9:1-9

6. See also Bamber Gascoigne, *The Christians* (London: Jonathan Cape Ltd., 1977) 12. Harvey Cox of Harvard Divinity School speaking from a legal perspective, commented:"[C]ourts [often] turn to some vague 'man-in-the-street' idea of what 'religion' should be. [But] a man-in-the-street approach would surely have ruled out early Christianity, which seemed both subversive and atheistic to the religious Romans of the day. The truth is that one man's 'bizarre cult' is another's true path to salvation, and the Bill of Rights was designed to safeguard minorities from the man-in-the-street's uncertain capacity for tolerance." *The New York Times,* Feb. 16, 1977, 25.

7. Genesis, 12:1; Joshua, 24: 2-3.

8. *Joint Statement of Opposition to Lasher Bill,* May 17, 1981, 3 (retained in Author's files.)

9. William James, *The Varieties of Religious Experience* (New York: Macmillan, 1961) 157-206. See also Henry S. Levinson, *The Religious Investigations of William James* (Chapel Hill: University of North Carolina Press, 1981) 112-113.

10. Paul E. Johnson, *Psychology of Religion* (Nashville: Abingdon, 1959) 129.

11. Ibid., 117.

12. Ibid., 129.

13. Albert C. Outler (ed.), *John Wesley* (New York: Oxford University Press, 1964) 274.

14. Sermon by Rev. Floyd H. Flake, Allen AME Church, Jamaica, N.Y., July 27, 1986. A Christian poster catalogue currently carries a poster which asks: "If you were accused of being a Christian, would there be enough evidence to prove it?" *1986 New Summer Posters,* Argus Communications.

15. Le Moult, supra, 602.

16. Luke, 18:22.

17. *United States v. Seeger,* 380 U.S., 163, 187 (1965).

18. *Welsh v. United States,* 398 U.S., 333, 358 (1970).

19. "Of Robots, Persons, and the Protection of Religious Beliefs," *Southern California Law Review,* Vol. 56, 1983. 1306.

20. Paul Tillich, *The Shaking of the Foundations* (New York: Scribner, 1948) 10-11.

21. Shapiro, supra, 1294.

22. Luke, 22:42.

23. See Lifton, *Thought Reform and the Psychology of Totalism,* supra, Chapter 22. Psychologist Lee Coleman suggests that Lifton's words about guilt manipulation "fit the situation of the imprisoned victim of 'deprogramming' far more closely than that of a religious recruit. Held in a motel room or perhaps the parents' home, the person is made to feel exquisitely guilty. He is made to feel that his current activities are a rejection of parents and family. In fact, the person may have no such hostile feelings towards his family, but in the setting of a deprogramming, only outright rejection of the 'cult' will satisfy the family and their hired helpers.

Another element of the manipulation of the person is the encouragement to deny responsibility for his choices. If only he will acknowledge that he is brainwashed and did not truly choose—by his own free will—to join the 'cult,' all will be forgiven. All family resentment will then be focused on the 'cult,' which is solely responsible for any disapproved behavior. This is too tempting for some persons to resist, and it is from such persons that the anti-cult movement recruits its crusading members." Lee Coleman, "New Religions and 'Deprogramming:' Who's Brainwashing Whom?" in Thomas Robbins, William C. Shepherd and James McBride (eds.), *Cults, Culture, and The Law* (Chico, CA: Scholars Press, 1985) 73.

24. Shapiro, supra, 1307-1308.

25. Robert J. Lifton, *Thought Reform and the Psychology of Totalism* (New York: Norton, 1961) 429. See also "Cultism: A Conference for Scholars and Policy Makers," held at Wingspread, Sept. 9-11, 1985, sponsored by The American Family Foundation, *et al.*, 3.

26. Thomas à Kempis, *The Imitation of Christ* (New York: Penguin, 1952) 45-46.

27. Ibid., 46-47.

28. Shapiro, supra, 1301, quoting F.D. Joret, *Dominican Life* (1937) 6.

29. F. Flinn, "Criminalizing Conversion," supra, 34. See also description of the Catholic lay organization "Opus Dei," "A Church Within the Church," *San Francisco Examiner* (San Francisco, CA), June 1, 1986, A-1.

30. Joseph H. Fichter, *The Holy Family of Father Moon* (Kansas City: Leaven Press, 1985) 40.

31. Matt, 5:48.

32. Reinhold Niebuhr, "Grace as Power in, and as Mercy towards, Man," in William E. Conn (ed.), *Conversion* (New York: Alba House, 1978) 28-29.

33. Outler, *John Wesley,* supra, 274.

34. Johnson, supra, 128.

35. Thomas McGowan, "Conversion: A Theological View" in Herbert Richardson (ed.), *New Religions and Mental Health,* supra, 129. In a subsequent article, McGowan expanded his view "that some of the principal beliefs of Unification theology are at least quite compatible with the theology set forth in the nineteenth century by Horace Bushnell." Thomas McGowan, "Horace Bushnell and the Unification Movement: A Comparison of Theologies," in Herbert Richardson (ed.), *Ten Theologians Respond to the Unification Church* (New York: Rose of Sharon, 1981) 21.

36. Richard De Maria, "A Psycho-Social Analysis of Religious Conversion" in M. Darrol Bryant and Herbert Richardson (eds.), *A Time for Consideration* (New York: The Edwin Mellen Press, 1978) 85. See also Albert C. Outler (ed.), *John Wesley* (New York: Oxford University Press, 1964) 55-56.

37. Ibid., 89.

38. McGowan, supra, 167-168.

39. De Maria, supra, 90.

40. Thomas Merton, *No Man is an Island* (New York: Harvest/HBJ, 1955) 112.

41. De Maria, supra, 90-91. See for example, Clarence H. Faust and Thomas H. Johnson (eds.), *Jonathan Edwards: Representative Selections* (New York: Hill and Wang, 1935). Jonathan Edwards strongly defended the powerful emotionalism of the Great Awakening because "the passions are the spring of conduct" and that "vital religion must consist chiefly in a holy exercise of them." Edwards insisted that the revivalist religious experience of the Great Awakening "was exactly the kind of religious expression which the supernatural sense bestowed by God's grace on the elect might be expected to bring forth." Ibid., xxxix.

42. Ibid, 91.

43. J. Gordon Melton and Robert L. Moore, *The Cult Experience* New York: Pilgrim, 1982) 56. David Bromley and Anson Shupe suggest a very similar analogy to the intensive indoctrination techniques used on Coast Guard cadets. See *Strange Gods,* supra, 95-96.

44. De Maria, supra, 94.

45. Ibid.

46. Eileen Barker, *The Making of a Moonie* (Oxford, New York: Basil Blackwell, 1984) 149.

47. Trudy Solomon, "Programming and Deprogramming the 'Moonies:' Social Psychology Applied," in David G. Bromley and James T. Richardson (eds.), *The Brainwashing/Deprogramming Controversy* (New York: Edwin Mellen, 1983) 179.

48. This is not to say that the Unification Church encourages or justifies such practice. To the extent that it has happened, it contradicts Church teaching in regard to families. See Chapter 9.

49. De Maria, supra, 95-96.

50. *Molko and Leal v. HSA,* 179 Cal. App. 3d 450, 472 (1986).

51. Johnson, supra, 127.

52. The Unification Church does not seek converts under the age of majority without parental consent.

53. Johnson, supra, 28.

54. Ibid., 127. See also William James, *The Varieties of Religious Experience,* supra, 185.

55. Kelley, supra, 28.

56. Universal Declaration of Human Rights. *adopted* Dec. 10, 1948, art. 2, G.A. Res. 217A, U.N. Doc. A/810, 71-72 (1948). See also De Socio, supra, 39.

57. Leo Pfeffer, "Equal Protection For Unpopular Sects," *Review of Law and Social Change,* Vol. 9, 1980-81,11.

58. Herbert Richardson, supra, xv. Gordon Melton and Robert Moore observe that: "If an interpreter of the new religious movements adopts the assumptions about conversion that view conversion as pathological by definition, then converts and devotees of the alternative religions will undoubtedly be assessed by such an interpreter as manifesting psychopathology. Another tendency we have noted is for psychological clinicians who have treated a number of current or former cult members in their psychotherapeutic practices to generalize on the basis of this inadequate sample and to conclude that experience of participation in the new religions is pathogenic. That this bad logic receives any credence is incredible. Using the same approach one could sample the persons in a psychiatrist's office at any given time, give them psychological tests, and on discovering psychopathology, conclude that going to a psychiatrist's office causes emotional disorders!" Melton & Moore, supra, 41.

59. James R. Lewis, "'Information Disease' and the Legitimation of Religious Freedom," presented at the annual meeting of the Association for the Sociology of Religion, Aug. 25-27, 1985, 3.

60. Shapiro, supra, 1309.

61. Robert N. Shapiro, "Mind Control or Intensity of Faith: The Constitutional Protection of Religious Beliefs," *Harvard Civil Liberties Review,* Vol. 13, 1978, 795.

Chapter 7

THE ROLE OF THE MEDIA

At the core of a democratic society is a free press. There is no question that the media play a critical role in preserving our freedoms. However, as much as their role is of tremendous importance to a free society, it is just as important for the media to uphold high ethical and journalistic standards and to avoid the temptation of sensationalism.[1] As this chapter will explain, the media have often fallen short, particularly in their reporting on the new religions.

The New Priesthood

The media have played an important role in shaping the opinions held by the general public with regard to new religions. The overriding factor is that the media have a special interest in this issue: to sell newspapers and to attract viewers. Jody Powell, press secretary to President Jimmy Carter, offers the incisive comment that the media have a tremendous "bias to make news reports interesting" because if they don't, their newspapers or broadcasts don't "sell". As Powell bluntly writes: "The fact is that news has to sell, or those who report it and edit it will find themselves searching for a new job." He calls "economics" the most likely motive "to promote deception and dishonesty."[2]

Certainly if sensationalism is the name of the game, the "cult-story" has had all the drama needed. Nearly all of the controversial issues are present: "religion, money, sex, family, exotic races, strange cultures, supposed conspiracies, white-hatted vigilantes, and resonances with America's Asian wars".[3]

The media pride themselves on their role as the courageous watchdog/ombudsman for society. Richard Grenier, who is a writer for *Commentary*, asserts that the American media constitute "a new self-appointed priesthood." Some of its members have also said they are the "custodian of our nation's 'virtue'."[4] Many, particularly in the religious community, are lamenting that the media have largely displaced the clergy as the moral guide for society.[5]

Of particular concern, as Jody Powell comments, is the fact that journalists have no one "looking over their shoulder."

They have complete freedom to report news as *they* see it without having to answer to anyone. Almost all of the checks on their performance are "located *within the organization.*" Powell adds, "the only judge of the performance of the *Washington Post* is the *Washington Post* -- or at least the only judge in a position to do much about it. The same is true for CBS News, *Time* magazine, and so on down the list."[6]

This view is echoed by many other notable figures. For instance, syndicated columnist William Rusher laments: "In the continuing battle for power in today's society, technology has put tremendous new weapons in the hands of a few unelected masterminds in the media."[7]

In an editorial following the verdict in *Sharon v. Time Inc.* in which a jury found that *Time* magazine had defamed Israeli Cabinet Minister Ariel Sharon in 1982, the *Los Angeles Times* acknowledged that this case raised "troublesome questions for journalism in general." The editorial candidly asked: "Is journalism sufficiently hospitable to outside ciriticism of its performance? Does it provide its critics with an adequate forum for their complaints? Is it sufficiently self-critical?"[8]

Religious Reporting

Religious figures have been particularly vulnerable to the tremendous power of the media. A survey of the national media elite conducted during 1979 and 1980 sheds some light on this. The survey was directed by Stanley Rothman and S. Robert Lichter, under the auspices of the Research Institute on International Change at Columbia University. They conducted hour-long interviews with 240 journalists and broadcasters at the most influential media outlets, including *The New York Times, The Washington Post, The Wall Street Journal, Time, Newsweek, U.S. News and World Report,* the news departments at CBS, NBC, ABC and PBS, and major public broadcasting stations.[9]

While not drawing any final conclusions, one of the most significant characteristics of the media elite that was discovered was its secular outlook. "Exactly 50 percent eschew any religious affiliation.... Very few are regular church goers. Only 8 percent go to church or synagogue weekly, and 86 seldom or never attend religious services."[10] Grenier goes so far as to comment: "...in short, the general atmosphere of the media elite is overwhelmingly secular when it is not frankly anti-religious."[11]

It is important to state that non-attendance at church, synagogue or mosque does not of itself disqualify one to report on religious activites, but it may make it easier to misunderstand religious beliefs and practices. In fact, there is an inherent difficulty in evaluating anyone's religious faith from outside. The courts have generally shied away from making such determinations, as the historic religious liberty case *United States v. Ballard* made clear. The media, however, have been less willing than the courts to defer to the sanctity of religious beliefs. There tends to be an overdose of skepticism on the part of the media when evaluating the veracity of the religious experience. They have generally failed to heed Supreme Court Justice Robert H. Jackson's admonition in his famous dissent in *Ballard*:

> *Such experiences, like some tones and colors, have existence for one, but none at all for another. They cannot be verified to the minds of those whose field of consciousness does not include religious insight. When one comes to trial which turns on any aspect of religious belief or representation, unbelievers among his judges are likely not to understand him and are almost certain not to believe him.*[12]

Justice Jackson went to great lengths to explain this dilemma and the great danger posed to religious liberty if non-believers are allowed to impose their judgment upon believers. He pointed out that religious faith itself is, by definition, an intangible theory. He quoted William James, one of the founders of modern psychology, who said: "Faith means belief in something concerning which doubt is still theoretically possible."[13] Jackson added: "Belief in what one may demonstrate to the senses is not faith. All schools of religious thought make enormous assumptions, generally on the basis of revelations authenticated by some sign or miracle."[14]

William James wrote that the vitality of religion lies in the religious experience. "If you ask what these experiences are, they are conversations with the unseen, voices and visions, responses to prayer, changes of heart, deliverance from fear, inflowings of help, assurances of support whenever certain persons set their own internal attitude in certain appropriate ways."[15] Justice Jackson further added: "The appeal in such matters is to a very different plane of credulity than is invoked by representations of secular fact."[16]

Justice Jackson was specifically concerned with the role of the courts in evaluating religions, yet his analysis is worthy of consideration by the media. Although the media have a public duty to serve as a watchdog over public institutions, they also have a duty to provide fair and truthful reporting. As will be shown, their reporting on the "cults" has frequently demonstrated a tremendous insensitivity to, and lack of understanding of, the beliefs and practices of new religious movements. What is quite evident is that the "cult story" has had too much appeal to be resisted. The media's handicap of often not being qualified to make judgments about the validity of religious beliefs or practices has not prevented them from taking advantage of sensationalism to sell their product.

Under these circumstances, it does not take a prophet to predict that a small, new, idealistic and zealous group of believers would receive a rather unsympathetic airing in the media.

Irresponsible Reporting

Before elaborating on the issue of biased reporting on new religious mevements, it might be worth adding that the situation would not be so bad if the media were simply poorly informed on religious issues. However, in all too many instances, the media have fallen prey to irresponsible reporting, and this pertains not just to media coverage of religious issues.

The *Sharon v. Time* case referred to earlier is but one prominent example. A further example is the experience of William Tavoulareas, retired president of Mobil Corporation. The agony of his legal battle with a media giant such as *The Washington Post* is vividly portrayed in Tavoulareas' book *Fighting Back*. He explains that he, like everyone else, had heard stories of media coverage of important subjects that was "often wildly biased and uninformed." However, he never imagined that it could happen to him:

> ***The Washington Post*** *was able to first print a series of lies about me and my son; then to absolutely refuse to retract those lies even after the* ***Post*** *knew its most serious accusations to be untrue; then to take a considerable portion of the savings I had in the world to make me vindicate my rights in court.... In complete contradiction to what I had always believed about what it means to be an American and to enjoy equality under the law, I found that the legal "facts" were that* ***The Washington Post*** *and its owners were not on the same legal footing as everyone else...*[17]

Tavoulareas expressed his hope that through his experience the American people could understand "just how confused and misbegotten the all-powerful media in this country have become." He believes that his case gave the public "the opportunity to see that a powerful, wealthy newspaper (thousands of times more wealthy that I am) can blithely assassinate a man's character even when it has clear warnings that its story is not true. I want the American people to see that certain elements of the media have become so arrogant that they simply do not care whether they wreck a man's life. In seeing that, I hope Americans will see that in the name of a free press, the freedom of everybody else has been severely abridged."[18]

A more famous case that has been called illustrative of "character assassination" by the media is that of CBS reporting of the "misdeeds" of General William Westmoreland during the Vietnam War. Although the 1985 trial was never completed, what became evident to some observers was that CBS had misled the public in its 1982 documentary "The Uncounted Enemy: A Vietnam Deception." Stephen Klaidman, a senior research fellow at the Kennedy Institute of Ethics at Georgetown University wrote:

> *CBS almost certainly misled viewers by reducing an extremely complex situation to an unrealistically simple thesis: that Westmoreland "cooked the books," conspiring to deceive the president about enemy troop*

A recently discovered photo taken by a UN photographer. It shows Rev. Moon carrying an injured disciple during his trek to the south after being liberated from a North Korean prison by United Nations forces in 1950.

[Courtesy Richard Lewis.]

The wedding of 2075 couples at Madison Square Garden, July 1, 1982.
[Courtesy Richard Lewis.]

Couples leaving the Madison Square Garden Wedding ceremony.
[Courtesy Richard Lewis]

Food and medical supplies are distributed to famine areas in Africa by the Church-sponsored International Relief Friendship Foundation (IRFF).
[Courtesy IRFF.]

Rev. Chung Hwan Kwak, head of foreign missions for the Unification Church, with missionaries.
[New Future Photo.]

Rev. and Mrs. Moon deep in prayer.
[Courtesy New Future Photo.]

Rev. Moon during his prison term at the Federal Correctional Institute in Danbury, Connecticut. Here he is in the kitchen with Takeru Kamiyama and Bo Hi Pak.
[Courtesy Richard Lewis.]

Rev. Moon testifies before the Senate Subcommittee on the Constitution Oversight Hearing on the State of Religious Liberty In America. June 26, 1984.
[New Future Photo.]

[13]
Ted Patrick leaving a police station.
[Courtesy New Future Photo.]

[14]
Mose Durst, President of the Unification Church in America, conducting a press conference after the U.S. Supreme Court refused to hear Rev. Moon's appeal of his tax conviction, May, 1984.
[Courtesy Richard Lewis.]

[5]
Senator Robert Dole conducting a hearing on the "cults" in 1979.
[Courtesy New Future Photo.]

[6]
Rev. Dean M. Kelley testified at the Dole anticult hearing on behalf of the American Civil Liberties Union.
[Courtesy Dean M. Kelley.]

[7]
Dr. John Clark testifying before Dole hearing.
[Courtesy New Future Photo.]

[3]
John Biermans with his parents, at a parents' seminar in Berkeley, California, April, 1979.
[From Author's personal album.]

[4]
Hannelore, Alicia and John Biermans.
[Courtesy Jonathan Gullery.]

strength so that he could continue pursuing an immoral and unwinnable war.

Even if you buy the CBS thesis, as some knowledgeable observers do, the question still arises: Why produce the show in such a one-sided way? Many of the participants in the situation described on the program took a very different view of the matter from the one presented by CBS Reports, and they were not heard on the air.

A common answer is that to be "good television" a documentary must have "impact"; that no effective program says, "On the one hand this, but on the other, that." The implication is that unless the show has impact, nobody will watch it.[19]

Some observers have suggested that the public bears some responsibility for sensationalist reporting. It is said that the media are simply responding to popular demand for "more than the world can give us." And it is for this reason that the public requires "that something be fabricated to make up for the world's deficiency."[20] In offering this hypothesis in his book *The Image,* Daniel J. Boostin writes that our "demand for illusions" has been a primary cause of a phenomenon which he called "pseudo-events." These are events that are only partially real but because they are photographed and reported in the media, they are given a force in the eyes of the public that is far beyond their actual significance.[21]

The Experience of the Unification Church

An important factor to consider is that the media often rely heavily on previous accounts in other newspapers or electronic media, without making independent efforts to verify the truth or accuracy of their statements. For example, during the early days of the Unification Church in South Korea, opponents of the church sought to create scandal by making allegations of illicit sexual activity. This was reported in Korean newspapers more than 30 years ago and, despite the fact that no evidence was ever produced of the improprieties alleged, this outrageous accusation still appears in newspapers throughout the world. A typical headline appeared in the *Chicago Tribune* on March 27, 1978, "Moon Church Traced from Sex Cult."[22] This allegation is particularly offensive since the immoral conduct described is anathema to the very core of Unification theology.[23]

Many Unification Church members over the years have been mystified at how the incredible stories of orgies and sexual practices of Rev. Moon and his church members could make headlines all over the world. It is not hard to see that if one false and outrageous headline in Seoul, Korea, can be repeated *ad nauseam* in other media throughout the world, then such a rumor can spread to the level of popular acceptance. Of course, it can happen more readily and blatantly when assisted by organized opponents of the Church.

This surprising media practice was confirmed by the experience of Philosophy Professor Frederick Sontag of Pomona College when we set out to conduct research on the Unification Church in 1976. He initially pulled together 122 clippings and as he read them, he expected "great revelations." Instead, he discovered that "give or take a few items, all the stories sounded alike, and the substance was really the same." Later, as he visited various Church centers throughout Europe and began to see a different side of the movement, he wrote:

> *I puzzled more and more over the uniformity and similarity of the press accounts. No doubt there are many explanations that could be given.* ***Newsweek*** *magazine had done extensive research for a comprehensive cover story, and, when I posed this puzzle about the uniformity of the press coverage, one of their editors explained the facts of newspaper and magazine life to me. Few writers and editors have the time, he said, for much extensive, on-site investigation, so they borrow from one another's stories. Once an account is printed, it tends to be repeated and believed just because it is in print. This phenomenon is not confined to "yellow journals" but applies to all media. When I pressed the editors of* ***Der Spiegel*** *about their source for one oft-repeated charge about Moon's early sex practices, they replied, as if it solved the mystery, 'But we read that in* ***The New York Times****!'*[24]

One of the most aggravating examples of media distortion about the Unification Church has involved the large wedding ceremonies. The image that has been conjured up by the media over the years has left many people with a strange and misleading perception about the Church. In his introduction to a sociological study of Unification Church marriages by James Grace, *Sex and Marriage in the Unification Movement*, Religion Professor Mac Linscott Ricketts observes:

> *For those whose knowledge of the recent mass weddings is limited to what they read in newspapers and magazines or see on their television screens, such happenings can only appear bizarre at best, or sinister and frightening at worst. Moreover, the media have, as a rule, been far from impartial in reporting on the activities of Rev. Moon, but on the contrary have served--intentionally or unintentionally--as vehicles for the views of a small but vigorously vocal "anti-cult movement" whose principal objective has been the discrediting of the Unification Church. But for one who, like Dr. Grace, is willing to take the trouble to go into matters in depth, the marriage practices of the Unificationists cease to be bizarre or sinister and are seen to be instead the focal point of an amazingly fertile and original theology.*[25]

The continual dissemination of unfounded accusations is a problem that lawyers of New York State recently addressed. At the 12th Annual Law and Press Conference sponsored by the New York State Bar Association, attorney Harold J. Boreanaz lamented: "I do not believe that the media truly believes in the concept of presumption of innocence or the burden of proof, these constitutional safeguards that we all hold dear."[26]

Gregory Tillett of the Department of Religious Studies at the University of Sydney in Australia conducted a research project concerning the media's treatment of the Unification Church. In his paper entitled "The Moonies, Media and Religious Persecution", he concludes:

> *The cases which have been considered are typical in both method and material, in what they say and what they fail to say, and in the way it is said. Either by partial representation, or misrepresentation, the media creates popular prejudice, perpetuates the prejudice it creates, and then reports on that prejudice and its effects. Its*

> *power to manipulate the minds of masses of people is far greater than it alleges even for Sun Myung Moon, and its use of this technique for the propagation of its aim of financial success exceeds even the business empire of his followers.*[27]

Tillett cites a series of examples of the built-in bias of the media. One example he describes in detail is a press campaign against the Unification Church in 1981 on the basis of one man's claims, and the "typical failure" of the media to investigate them. It involved a 20-year-old Perth woman, Angela Hamersley, who had been abducted and committed to a psychiatric hospital by a group of professional "deprogrammers" employed by her parents. Tillett explains that the local press reported the case with headlines reading: "Fight with cult costs $13,000" and "Cults brainwash, says girl's father." He adds that "even when the headline was vaguely neutral ("Perth Moonie girl criticizes parents' action") the story which followed left no doubt who was right and who was wrong. The only people given any exposure in the media were the parents (strongly anti-Moonie), the local leader of an anti-cult group (strongly anti-Moonie), another ex-Moonie..."[28]

The media gave Ms. Hamersley very little space to tell her own story. Hidden amidst the overwhelming hostility was her statement that she had intended leaving the church and was returning to Australia anyway. She denied being brainwashed or losing her free will, and she opposed and objected to the action her parents had taken. "The media reported these comments -- and immediately sought her father's assessment of them; he simply implied that the effects of her brainwashing had not fully worn away, and the media clearly gave all credence to him (supported by the local anti-cult man) and none to the daughter."[29]

Tillett goes on to describe the background of Ms Hamersley's commitment to the psychiatric hospital. It had been arranged "on the basis of two sworn affidavits, one from her father (who had not seen her for nine months), and the other from a physician (not a psychiatrist) who had never seen her at all!"[30] Furthermore, the hospital denied the girl access to her attorney or a minister or psychiatrist of her choice.[31] Nevertheless, she was subjected to repeated and regular visits (against which she protested, but to no avail) from a professional "deprogrammer" (with no medical qualifications) who was then under criminal indictment for kidnapping in California.

Tillett explains that later, the media *"did* report the very selective, somewhat inaccurate, and wholly incomplete story presented by the girl's father and his supporters." Tillett adds: "Thus the Moonies were shown to be dangerous, cruel and sinister. Presumably even had they bothered to check the facts, the media would have found fraudulent committal to a psychiatric hospital less dangerous, cruel and sinister."[32]

This type of unbalanced reporting has also been documented by a Canadian religion professor, M. Darrol Bryant, in an article, "Media Ethics: The Elimination of Perspective." He describes in detail a documentary, "Moonstruck," shown on the Canadian Broadcasting Corporation (CBC) program "fifth estate" in the autumn of 1976 concerning the Unification Church. Bryant had been interviewed about this study of the Unification Church by the CBC. After the interview, he had given them various scholarly publications about the Unification Church and suggestions of people within the Church and within the academic community who could provide information. Much to his chagrin, what actually appeared on this major national program was, as he terms it, "the elimination of perspective", namely, any positive opinion of the Unification Church. Bryant asks:

> *What then of the seeming open-mindness presented by the researcher? Was there willful duplicity here? Had the content of the show already been determined? Was the researcher simply looking for additional confirmation or further ammunition for attack?*
>
> *Regardless of the answers to these questions, it is clear that we did not get a program on the controversial Unification Church. By the time the show was presented, the controversy had been resolved within the staff of the* **fifth estate**. *In the perspective of the program there is no controversy: the group is simply dangerous and bad. Anyone viewing the program would be left with the*

> *impression that there is no other perspective than the one presented. Indeed how could there be another perspective on such a reprehensible group? Here is where the lie is exposed. Rather than providing the viewer with information and a range of opinion that would allow the viewer to make his own determination, the* **fifth estate** *decided the question in advance. Having already determined that the Unification Church is essentially evil and pernicious, they simply selected and framed their material in ways that would confirm their original bias.*[33]

One former Unification Church member, journalist David Hulme, contends that "'reputable journalists' have pulled some of the most dishonest stunts imaginable in the scramble for 'good stories' that increase suspicion of the church. The bulk of printed stories I've seen over the years tended to deepen public ignorance of the church rather than dissipate it."[34] Canadian journalist Bart Testa suggests that some journalists wrote newspaper accounts about the Unification Church that could not be considered "presenting news." Instead, they transformed "news into advertising" to persuade the public that the "Moonies" were the bad guys and anti-cultists, especially deprogrammers, were the heroes.[35]

Are All Cults the Same?

One of the specific problems that arises from the media's distorted reporting is that all of the small new religious groups are lumped together in the same category as "the cults." As Harvey Cox observes, these religious movements "differ from each other so fundamentally that stuffing them all in the cult basket makes no sense whatever."[36]

This is distressing because Unification Church members, for instance, are accused of a myriad of practices which have absolutely no basis of fact in the Unification Church. Accusations range from shaving of heads, suicide pacts and promiscuous sexual practices. These particular practices can be traced to the following groups: shaving of heads is done by the Hare Krishna Movement; members of the People's Temple took part in a suicide pact in 1979; and the accusation of promiscuous sexual practices apparently derived rom the activities of the Children of God and the Rajneesh organization. Again, the issue regarding sexual practices is particularly upsetting to Unification Church members since church teachings absolutely forbid any sexual interaction outside of the marriage relationship. Also, Unification theology strongly condemns suicide.[37]

What must be clearly understood is that a new religious movement in and of itself is not necessarily good or evil. A group may have a very good purpose or it may have an evil purpose. Some are clearly *not* good. This book does not purport to be a defense of the beliefs or practices of all groups nor does it pass judgment on any.

Religious studies professor Ronald B. Flowers of Texas Christian University makes a similar point in an attempt to clarify the confusion surrounding the terms "cult" and "sect." He says that the terms themselves are neutral; "they carry no value judgment. The media have done a great disservice in perpetuating the commonly held idea that cults are always and necessarily evil. That is just not true. A cult is inherently neither good nor evil, it is just different."[38]

Cox explains further that a brief look at some of the groups usually labelled as "cults" should automatically raise questions about the label itself. Cox writes that the Hare Krishna movement represents a centuries-old Indian devotional tradition and that the Unification Church blends elements of East Asian folk religion, American civil religion, and latter-day Calvinism. Scientology, on the other hand, is the "imaginative invention of an ingenious science fiction writer," L. Ron Hubbard. Finally, he asserts, "People's Temple had almost nothing in common with any of the above."[39]

On this same note, sociologist Joseph Fichter writes that the Jonestown tragedy had the powerful effect of fixing the pejorative concept of the "cult" in the popular mind. This was accomplished courtesy of the "the news media's lurid accounts of the final tragedy of Reverend Jim Jones and his People's Temple. 'Perhaps...journalists used the cult terminology in the hope that a label would suffice where an explanation was unavailable'."[40]

Present Rhetoric Compared with Past Rhetoric

Herbert Richardson of the University of Toronto compares the media rhetoric against the Unification Church with the rhetoric used earlier against the Catholics and the Jews.[41] He cites Ray Billington who, in *The Protestant Crusade 1800-1860*, describes in vivid detail the intensity of the public outcry against the Catholic Church because of the widespread reporting of Catholic "atrocities" -- nearly all of which were later proven to be totally false. Billington quotes several examples of anti-Catholic literature, including such titles as "Priests, Prisons and Women; or a consideration of the question as to whether unmarried foreign priests ought to be permitted to erect prisons into which, on the pretence of religion, they seduce, entrap or by force compel young women to enter and, after they are in, to secure their property, keep them in confinement and to compel them as their slaves to submit themselves to their will under the penalty of flogging or the dungeon."[42]

Richardson explains that journals of all kinds sought to outdo themselves in reporting Catholic atrocities. The public was so provoked by the lurid media accounts of alleged Catholic practices that, in certain cases, vigilante groups broke into religious houses in order to liberate the young novices who were supposedly held captive there. "A perverse power to enslave the young was attributed to the Catholic clergy -- especially Jesuits -- who were accused of playing on the superstitions and credulity of the young."[43]

Tillett asserts that "To become a Moonie is both evil and dangerous, not because it is really any different from becoming anything else, but because the media defines the Moonies as evil in 1982, just as they defined the Mormons as evil in 1922, and the Roman Catholics as a threat to the world in 1892."[44] He adds that because the average person does not have access to accurate information nor the inclination to do the research, the media controls the flow of facts and thereby directs and manipulates public opinion. "The media creates heroes and villains on the basis of its selection and manipulation of the facts. And villains sell more than heroes. Unspeakable evils, when spoken of in dark hints and suggestive innuendoes, are good for attracting customers."[45]

Movements: Genesis, Exodus, and Numbers. He expresses his amazement at how the media have uncritically accepted "magical notions of mind control." He adds:

> *"While it is not surprising to find absurd claims about cultist mind control in sensationalist tabloids...it is astonishing to find them certified by expert social scientists--or at least by people with advanced degrees whom the media present as experts. It also seems odd that the media, usually so eager to reveal dirty secrets, fail to discover that some of their experts on religious movements are poorly regarded by others in the field, while most are held in no regard at all, since they have never participated in the field."*[54]

The effect of such distorted media coverage is difficult to assess fully. Yet it is quite clear that the sheer volume of hostile stories, which gained greater credibility with each telling, served as a serious handicap to advancing the cause of the Unification Church.[55] They tainted everything the Church sought to do, and it is only within the last three or four years that the climate has begun to change.[56]

Ray Billington makes a similar point in regard to the Catholic experience:

> *Discredited as she may have been in her later years, Maria Monk's books continued to enjoy unstinted popularity; the three hundred thousand copies of* ***Awful Disclosures*** *sold prior to the Civil War and the editions which have appeared since that time justly earned for it the questionable distinction of being the 'Uncle Tom's Cabin of Know-Nothingism.' The immediate effect of this volume, however, was to demonstrate both the profits and influence of sensational propaganda. Much of the wave of publication which followed with such telling effect in the creation of anti-Catholic sentiment can be attributed to the widely read and accepted* ***Awful Disclosures.***[57]

Just as the Catholic Church recovered from those dark days, the Unification Church appears to be recovering as well. The earlier misunderstanding and horrific stereotypes that were created have begun to give way to a fuller awareness of the true nature of the Church. It is precisely such studies as those done by Bromley, Shupe, Van Driel, James T. Richardson, Herbert Richardson, Tillett, Bryant, Fichter, Wallis and others which provide the information and clarification that have been so sorely needed. With a more balanced view offered by the media, the many heartaches and misunderstandings of the past can finally come to an end.

References

1. See, for example, "Sounds Like Heartburn", *People*, Sept. 8, 1986, 132.

2. Jody Powell, *The Other Side of the Story*, (New York: William Morrow, 1984) 15.

3. Herbert Richardson, supra, xxvi.

4. Richard Grenier, "The New Priesthood", presented to the Seventh World Media Conference, Tokyo, Japan, Nov. 19-22, 1984, 1 (retained in author's files).

5. Ibid.

6. Powell, supra, 19.

7. William Rusher, "The Stakes are high in Sharon, Westmoreland case against the press," *New York Tribune* (New York, NY), Nov. 27, 1984. See also William C. Westmoreland, "Court is Not the Best Forum", *The Los Angeles Daily Journal* (Los Angeles, CA), February 26, 1985.

8. "Behind the Sharon Verdict", *Los Angeles Times* (Los Angeles, CA), Jan. 27, 1985.

9. S. Robert Lichter and Stanley Rothman, "The Media Elite and American Value", Ethics and Public Policy Center, No. 38, April 1982, 42.

10. Ibid., 43.

11. Grenier, supra, 3.

12. *U.S. v. Ballard,* 322 U.S. 78, 93 (1944).

13. William James, *The Will to Believe* (New York: Dover, 1960) 90.

14. *U.S. v. Ballard,* 94.

15. William James, *Collected Essays and Reviews*, 427-28, cited in *U.S. v. Ballard*, 94.

16. *U.S. v. Ballard*, 94.

17. "Mobil Official Bares Anguish of Post Battle", *Washington Times* (Washington, DC), April 22, 1986. Tavoulareas successfully argued his case before a jury but was later reversed by an appeals court. As he discovered, it is almost impossible to win a libel case against the media if one is a public figure, unless malice can be proven.

18. Ibid.

19. Stephen Klaidman, "CBS is Not Blameless", *The Los Angeles Daily Journal*, (Los Angeles, CA), Feb. 26, 1985. Klaidman had previously worked for *The New York Times*, *The Washington Post* and *The International Herald Tribune*. See also "Westmoreland Takes on CBS", *Newsweek*, Oct. 22, 1984, 60.

20. Daniel J. Boorstin, *The Image: A Guide to Pseudo-Events in America* (New York: Antheum, 1973) 9.

21. Ibid., 38-39.

22. This particular article stated that Rev. Moon's group "interprets the Bible in sexual terms." This, of course, is partially true since the Unification Church teaches that the Fall of Man involved a sexual crime. However, this hardly makes the Unification Church a "sex cult". The remarkable aspect of these allegations of sexual improprieties is that they are so similar to those made against Catholics, Mormons and others as discussed in Chapter 1. See also David Brion Davis, supra. It makes one wonder if it is not the "teller" of these "tales" who has the obsession with sex.

23. See James H. Grace, *Sex and Marriage in the Unification Movement* (New York: Edwin Mellen, 1984) vii.

24. Frederick Sontag, *Sun Myung Moon and the Unification Church* (Nashville: Abingdon, 1977) 20-21.

25. Grace, supra, v.

26. "Airing Concerns at Law and the Press Conference", *State Bar News*, (New York State Bar Association) June, 1986.

27. Gregory Tillett, "The Moonies, the Media, and Religious Persecution" (unpublished, retained in author's files), 1982, 12.

28. Ibid.

29. Ibid., 11-12.

30. Ibid., 12.

31. The author can confirm this because he personally received frantic phone calls from Ms. Hamersley, pleading aid so as to be released.

32. Ibid. The effect of media presentations of the Unification Church on relationships between its members and their parents cannot be overstated. Parents themselves, in a survey conducted by Hexel and Berger for the German government, blamed the media for much of the difficulty of dialogue with their children. Thus, the level of conflict in families "...is strongly influenced by the public debate. Each lessening of the conflicts between NRM [New Religious Movements] and church and public sector also affects positively the familial interaction. Parents also admitted that by being influenced by public opinion they were reacting wrongly. They complained about the slanderous media coverage...this made dialogue with their child impossible and also out of this grew a social discrimination for them in their environment." [This is an unofficial translation.] See Herbert Berger and Peter C. Hexel, *Ursachen und Wirkungen gesellschaftlicher Verweigerung junger Menschen unter besonderer Berucksichtigung der "Jugendreligionen"* (Vienna, 1981).

33. M. Darrol Bryant, "Media Ethics: The Elimination of Perspective." in Herbert Richardson (ed.), *New Religions and Mental Health* (New York: Edwin Mellen, 1980) 72-

73. See also journalist Bart Testa's article on this same program, "It Would Have Been Nice To Hear From You...On fifth estate's 'Moonstruck'" in H. Richardson, supra. Testa writes: "I think the failure of 'Moonstruck' as a documentary film, though particularly extreme, is typical of the media's failure to deal with the Moonies, not only on the moral level of 'objectivity' but on the level of pleasure as well." Ibid., 80.

34. David Hulme, "Substance and Shadow", *The Journal of the Foreign Correspondents Club of Japan*, Feb. 15, 1983, 8.

35. See Bart Testa, "Making Crime Seem Natural: The Press and Deprogramming" in *A Time For Consideration*, supra, 45-46, 76-79.

36. Harvey Cox, Introduction to David Bromley and Anson Shupe, *Strange Gods* (Boston: Beacon Press, 1981) xiii.

37. See Peter Gogan, "Is Life Worth Living? Youth Suicide and its Prevention", *Front Line*, Vol. 3, no. 1, 1986, 77.

38. Ronald B. Flowers, *Religion In Strange Times: The 1960's and 1970's* (Mercer University Press, 1984) 109.

39. Ibid.

40. Fichter, *The Holy Family of Father Moon*, supra, 12, quoting Gillian Lindt, "Journeys to Jonestown", *Union Seminary Quarterly Review*, Fall/Winter, 1981-82. This "lumping" together is usually fed to the media by anti-cultists who can paint a much more hysterical picture when they lump all of the offenses or alleged offenses of dozens of groups under the heading of practices by "cults". For instance, there have been a number of incidents of child neglect or child abuse by several groups in the United States over the past few years. Now this has become one more item on a list of "cult-related concerns" that applies indiscriminantly to all the "cults" in reports published by the American Family Foundation. There has also been much concern in recent years about the "Satan worshippers" or "Satanists" and, of course, these

people are also lumped in under the same general rubric of "cults". The anti-cultists never bother to point out that Satan worship is absolutely abhorrent to most of the other groups in the "cult basket". See generally, "Cultism", AFF report, supra.

41. See Chart, page 84.

42. Billington, supra, 361.

43. Richardson, supra, xxvi.

44. Tillett, supra, 5.

45. Ibid.

46. David G. Bromley and Anson D. Shupe, Jr., *The New Vigilantes* (Beverly Hills: Sage, 1980) 170.

47. Ibid., 172.

48. Ibid. This actual pattern is supported by the research of E.J. Epstein in his 1975 book, *Between Fact and Fiction: The Problem of Journalism,* (New York: Vintage, 1975).

49. Roy Wallis, *Sectarianism: Analysis of Religious and Non-Religious Sects* (London: Peter Owen, 1975) 92.

50. Barend van Driel and James T. Richardson, "Cult Versus Sect: Categorization of New Religious Movements in the American Print Media", presented at the annual meeting of the Association for the Sociology of Religion, New York, NY, Aug. 1986, 19.

51. Leo Pfeffer, in Herbert Richardson, (ed.), *Constitutional Issues in the Case of Rev. Moon,* supra, 542.

52. Van Driel and Richardson, supra, 18-19.

53. C.H. Weiss, "Media Report Card for Social Science", *Society,* March/April 1985, 40.

54. Rodney Stark, (ed.), *Religious Movements: Genesis, Exodus, and Numbers* (New York: Paragon House, 1985) 2-5.

55. Bromley and Shupe, *The New Vigilantes,* 173.

56. See, e.g., "Unification Church Gains Acceptance", *The New York Times,* (New York, NY), July 21, 1984; "After Controversy Surrounding Moon, Unification Church Gaining Acceptance", *The Evening Post* (Charleston, SC), Sept. 19, 1985.

57. Billington, supra, 108.

Chapter 8

THE LEGAL ASSAULT ON THE UNIFICATION CHURCH: WHAT THE COURTS HAVE SAID

The Unification Church has defended itself from a host of legal challenges over the years with significant success, and in the process it has forged a bond with other formerly "suspect" groups that now provides greater protection for the religious liberty of all religions.[1] Some legal scholars have suggested that the Unification Church is following the tradition of such religious groups as the Jehovah's Witnesses, the Seventh-Day Adventists, the Mormons and others who endured many years of legal challenges and, in the process, helped to create some of America's most significant legal pronouncements upon the sanctity and overriding importance of religious freedom.[2]

To a significant extent, the legal assault on the Unification Church has been a direct consequence of the prejudice described in earlier chapters. Because of the attacks by the anti-cult network and apostate members, with generous assistance from the media, the Unification Church and other new religions have been required to defend themselves on a broad range of legal fronts. For example, there have been lawsuits by former members who have attempted to literally extort large sums of money because of their former membership. Although it would be unthinkable for an ex-Catholic or ex-Methodist to bring such lawsuits, the much-maligned new religious movements have been forced to direct vast amounts of their resources away from their ministries to defend themselves in the legal arena. Fortunately, they do not have to face the lions as the early Christians did in the Roman "arenas," but the majority of the lawsuits are likewise a direct manifestation of the ingrained prejudice of society. A tax fraud trial is certainly a much more "civilized" version of persecution than burning at the stake or crucifixion, but the essential motive is the same.

Much of the relatively brief history of the Unification Church worldwide can be said to have been a history of struggle, persecution, perseverance and growth. This growth has usually come at great cost and sacrifice, but according to Unification theology such is the course of history. The many periods of challenge and struggle have been followed repeatedly by ultimate vindication. During research for his book on the Unification Church during the mid-1970s,

Frederick Sontag said one attorney had told him that the Church would usually lose the skirmishes on the lower trial court level but that higher courts would eventually see the constitutional issues at stake and reverse the tide. To a large extent, this is what has happened.

Disaffected Members' Claims

A recent vindication came with the March 31, 1986 decision of the California Court of Appeal in *Molko and Leal v. Holy Spirit Association for the Unification of World Christianity (HSA).*[3] As mentioned briefly in Chapter 3, this case involved allegations by two apostate members who had undergone abduction from the Church and as a result had recanted their beliefs. They made claims of brainwashing, deception, false imprisonment and intentional infliction of emotional distress. The Court of Appeal ruled that none of these charges justified a trial.

The plaintiffs, David Molko and Tracy Leal, did not dispute that to all outward appearances their decisions to join and participate in the Church were voluntary. Nor did they dispute the bona fides of the Unification Church's religious beliefs which they acknowledged they sincerely adopted as their own.[4] However, based on the testimony of psychologist Margaret Singer and psychiatrist Samuel Benson, they claim that their decisions were the result of "coercive persuasion." Singer and Benson offered their "expert" opinion that Molko and Leal joined as a result of the "systematic manipulation of social and psychological influences." Borrowing freely from studies of the victims of "brainwashing" in the Korean War, these "experts" gave a "scientific" interpretation of the Church's traditional religious practices (practices common to virtually every religion, old and new.) These were not really religious practices at all, they opined, but "techniques" utilized to produce "mental breakdowns."[5]

Their psychological "analysis" of a few of the Church's religious practices is revealing. From their perspective, traditional conceptions of heaven, hell and punishment for sin are *in reality* threats of force and the manipulation of guilt and fear used to coerce the novice. Chanting, fasting, prayer and proselytization are *in reality* mentally debilitating processes contrived to occupy time, weaken resistance and stifle critical thought. The traditional call to focus all activities and efforts on God is *in reality* nothing more than a clever means to isolate the adherent from the outside world. The teaching that non-believers cannot achieve salvation is *in reality* a technique to alienate a convert from family, friends and others who might cause the believer to question his faith.[6]

In the lower court, Judge Stuart Pollak emphatically rejected the validity of this testimony. The judge noted that Singer and Benson had never even examined the plaintiffs until long after their involvement with the Unification Church and that neither plaintiff had ever been restrained by the Church or its members.[7]

In a far-reaching opinion, the Court of Appeal agreed, holding that plaintiffs' "mind control" evidence was constitutionally repugnant and not admissible. The Court concluded that the "expert opinions" lacked any scientific basis. More importantly, the Court reasoned, when stripped of its scientific terminology, the opinions are nothing more than "veiled value judgments concerning the entire outlook of the Unification Church." The Free Exercise Clause of the First Amendment prohibits a court from inquiring into the motivations of believers. According to the Court, "When the Court is asked to determine whether conversion to the Church was induced by faith or by coercive persuasion, is it not in turn investigating and questioning the validity of that faith?"[8]

In the Court's view, the pseudo-scientific explanation of Singer and Benson "ignores the religious aspect of the Church's teachings and the spiritual nature of its hold on its members." As long as the constitution guarantees the free practice of religion, a *bona fide* church may not be summoned to answer the charges of former members that the church was so persuasive that they lost their ability to assent. Quoting Supreme Court Justice William O. Douglas, the Court concluded that: "Religious experiences which are as real as life to some may be incomprehensible to others. Yet the fact that they may be beyond the ken of mortals does not mean that they can be made suspect before the law."[9]

The Court also rejected plaintiffs' claims for emotional distress. According to the Court, "If threats (of the sort alleged by plaintiffs) were actionable, litigation against religious entities by former believers would be unconstrained and rampant."[10] Such "threats," said the Court, are not unique to the Unification Church and are protected by the First Amendment.

Dealing with allegations of deception by Unification Church members, the Court stated:

> *Plaintiffs' own testimony eliminates any triable issue of fact in this regard. Referring to the testimony of plaintiffs at deposition, the trial court observed that, "[b]y their own admissions, plaintiffs agreed to join the group because their association satisfied personal concerns and anxieties both were experiencing." The admissions that they joined the group for reasons which were not dependent upon its formal affiliations were buttressed, the court found, by the fact that "when [plaintiffs] learned the group was part of the Unification Church, they did not leave or attempt to leave, although they knew they might have done so. Their actions reflect that it was not their unawareness of defendant's affiliation that caused them to stay."*[11]

The Court further stated:

> *There is no competent evidence [that] either plaintiff was compelled to join the Unification Church or prevented from leaving. To the contrary, plaintiffs were at all times free to maintain contact with non-members, as they did, and to end their involvement with the Church and repudiate its teachings, as eventually they also did. The techniques used to recruit and indoctrinate plaintiffs...are not materially different from those employed by other organizations.*[12]

The decision in *Molko and Leal v. HSA* was built from the foundation of an earlier case won by the Unification Church, *Katz v. Superior Court* in 1977. In that case, San Francisco Superior Court Judge Lee Vavuris entered orders appointing parents as temporary conservators of five adult members of the Unification Church in order to permit "deprogramming" of the conservatees from ideas allegedly instilled by the Unification Church. The five conservatees petitioned for reversal by the California Court of Appeal. This appeal was ultimately successful.

The orders of the lower court purported to rely on a California conservatorship statute which was designed to conserve the property of persons found not to be competent to look after their own affairs, usually elderly persons who, according to the statute are "likely to be deceived or imposed upon by artful or designing persons." In such instances, the statute allowed a court to appoint a guardian or conservator. The appeals court held that it was a violation of these adults' constitutional right to religious freedom for the lower court to appoint their parents as their temporarary conservators for purposes of "deprogramming" them . The lower court had not found the conservatees to be insane, incompetent or unable to manage their property, which were the only grounds upon which guardians could be appointed. Thus, the court of appeal ruled that the evidence presented in the case did *not* justify the appointment of conservators of these religious adherents.[13]

Legal commentator John Le Moult explains further: "For the practices of a religious group to be regulated, they must pose 'some substantial threat to public safety, peace or order.' The Court found no such grounds for governmental regulation in the case of the voluntary religious conversion of the followers of Rev. Moon." [14]The Court stated: "We conclude that in the absence of such actions as render the adult believer himself gravely disabled as defined in the law of this state, the processes of this state cannot be used to deprive the believer of his freedom of action and to subject him to involuntary treatment."[15]

The Appellate Division of the Supreme Court of New York announced an important ruling dealing with related issues on September 2, 1986 in *Meroni v. Holy Spirit Association.*[16] This case involved another attempt to hold the Unification Church liable for the alleged brainwashing of its adherents. In a unanimous ruling, the appeals court rejected the notion of brainwashing as applied to Unification Church religious practices and dismissed the lawsuit.

The suit was brought by the father of a college student who attended a Unification Church weekend retreat some months prior to committing suicide. The court issued an unequivocal repudiation of claims that the Church 's recruitment techniques were anything but "common and accepted proselytizing practices." Speaking for the court, Justice James N. Niehoff stated that the conduct on the part of the Unification Church

> *which the plaintiff seeks to classify as tortious, constitutes common and accepted religious proselytizing practices, e.g., fasting, chanting, physical exercises, cloistered living, confessions, lectures, and a highly structured work and study schedule. To the extent that the plaintiff alleges that the decedent was "brainwashed" as a result of the Church's program, this claim must be viewed in the context of the situation as a whole, i.e., as a method of religious indoctrination that is neither extreme nor outrageous when it is considered that the subjects of the so-called "brainwashing" are voluntarily participating in the program, and the various activities mentioned above, which allegedly induced the "mind-control," are not considered by our society to be beyond all possible bounds of decency.*[17]

The opinion repeatedly rejected the concept of brainwashing as a basis for legal action. The Court added: "The claim of brainwashing is based upon the activities heretofore described, which, as previously noted, are commonly used by religious and other groups, and are accepted by society as legitmate means of indoctrination."[18]

Deprogramming Litigation

In another type of litigation, Unification Church members who were subjected to deprogrammings have brought lawsuits against their abductors in an attempt to establish legal safeguards against such gross violations of their religious and civil liberties. One such case was *Colombrito v. Kelly.*[19] In that case, the United States Court of Appeals for the Second Circuit rebuked the illegal practice of "deprogramming" or faithbreaking of Unification Church members. The case involved a lawsuit brought by Church member Tony Colombrito against deprogrammer Galen Kelly who had abducted him, held him against his will and subjected him to abuse, harassment and ridicule in an attempt to force him to recant his religious beliefs.

During the course of the trial, Colombrito decided to discontinue the lawsuit after Kelly's attorneys had forced Rev. Moon to take the witness stand. Instead of a trial dealing with the illegal activities of the kidnappers, trial judge Richard Owen allowed it to be turned into an inquisition of the Unification Church. A great deal of testimony on unsubstantiated allegations about the Church, all of which had no relevance to the issues at trial, aside from its prejudicial impact, was allowed. In the words of one commentator, Thomas Robbins, the trial judge "appears to have collaborated with the defense strategy of putting the Unification Church on trial 'to an unusual degree.'"[19*]

After the trial was discontinued, Kelly's attorneys requested attorney's fees and costs, claiming that the lawsuit by Colombrito had been groundless, frivolous and without merit. How anyone could argue that someone who had been subjected to the kind of abuse endured by Colombrito did not have a legitimate claim is difficult to imagine. Nevertheless, Judge Owen predictably agreed with Kelly and ordered the Unification Church to pay him in excess of $84,000 plus interest at 9% from May, 1982.

This, too, was a case of defeat at the lower court level and ultimate vindication in the higher courts, which have historically shown a greater sensitivity to constitutional rights. During oral argument and in the opinion itself, the Second Circuit was clearly incredulous that Kelly had the audacity to come before the Court under such circumstances.

In a unanimous ruling, the Court reversed Judge Owen's decision and awarded costs to the Unification Church. Judge Walter R. Mansfield, writing for the Court, traced the case law of the subject of attorney's fees in civil rights cases and found that Colombrito's action could not be judged groundless:

> *Indeed, he stood a reasonable chance of inducing a court to find that Kelly's actions were based on an anti-religious animus directed at the Unification Church. Colombrito's mother had obtained a New Jersey state court guardianship order without complying with clear*

> *statutory prerequisities for such an order. Kelly and his cohorts...had forcibly abducted the 27-year-old Colombrito. They held him against his will and made efforts to 'deprogram' him, i.e., to induce him to abandon his religious beliefs....As one court [the Tenth Circuit Court of Appeals] said of such 'deprogrammers' using such tractics:*
>
> > *[C]ertainly their conduct is odious and has the effect of depriving the victim of important rights—his liberty, his freedom, his right to practice his religion among other rights.*[20]

One of Kelly's defenses was that he had not acted out of any hatred or animosity towards the Unification Church. This was in response to one of Colombrito's claims that Kelly had violated Section 1985(3) of the Civil Rights Act which requires a "class-based animus." Judge Owen ruled that Colombrito failed to meet the requirements of the federal statute because he had acknowledged during his testimony that he felt his parents believed they were acting in his best interests.

The Second Circuit found Kelly's argument unpersuasive and Judge Owen's ruling erroneous. Judge Mansfield asserted:

> *Parental concern and a class-based animus may co-exist or indeed sometimes merge. It could reasonably be inferred from the present record that, although the parents acted out of concern for their son's well-being, they simultaneously were motivated by an intense animosity toward the Unification Church, to which he had been converted, and toward its beliefs and practices. Whether or not their appraisal of the Church's beliefs was sincere and shared by others, this gave them no right to seek out and combine with Kelly forcibly to deprive their 27-year-old adult son (not shown in any way to be mentally incompetent) of the right freely to move about, to adopt his own lifestyle, and to practice the religion he chose...His right to do so is the very core of the First and Fourteenth Amendments.*[21]

Investigations of the Church

The deprogramming/faithbreaking legal battle is only one of the many challenges the church has faced in the United States over the years.[22] There have been investigations by the Federal government, most notably the House Subcommittee on International Organizations during 1977-78 led by then Representative Donald Fraser of Minnesota. Ultimately, Fraser spent $685,000 in government funds and 18 months of his subcommittee's time, but failed to prove any allegation[23] made against Rev. Moon or the Unification Church.[24] Nevertheless, substantial damage was done by the media coverage of this investigation and today it is still not uncommon for the non-existent "findings" of this congressional investigation to be touted during testimony against the Unification Church.

Another apparent source of the pervasive mischaracterizations of Rev. Moon and the Unification Church has been the numerous state legislative investigations conducted in the 1970s.[25] During that time, state legislatures convened committee hearings to study the "cult problem," particularly focusing on Rev. Moon and the Unification Church. Prompted by anti-cult groups, the legislators dutifully heard a carefully orchestrated parade of former members of religious groups who had been coercively deprogrammed into abandoning their faith. Testimony at one of the first hearings (in Vermont) provided almost the entire basis for the controversial legal thesis of the anti-cult movement, "Religious Totalism: Gentle and Ungentle Persuasion under the First Amendment" by Richard Delgado.[26] This in turn has provided much of the foundation for New York and other state legislation which sought to legalize coercive deprogramming.[27]

Similar investigations have been conducted in Ohio (1977), Alabama (1978), Connecticut (1979), Massachusetts (1979), and New York (1979). Investigations have also carried into the 1980s, as is thoroughly documented in a recent article entitled "Criminalizing Conversion: The Legislative Assault on New Religions et al," by theologian Frank Flinn.[28]

Fortunately, defenders of religious liberty have spoken out to put a stop to these "investigations." In an article entitled "New Religions and the First Amendment," James E. Wood, Jr., editor of the *Journal of Church and State* described the concern of major church officials to a congressional hearing on religious "cults" in 1979. These officials, who represented such groups as the Baptist Joint Committee, the Lutheran Council, the National Council of Churches, the Synagogue Council of America, the United Methodist Church and the United Presbyterian Church, stated that their opposition was based on their concern that all of the witnesses scheduled "appear to have definite positions in support of regulation of 'cult' activity or efforts to 'deprogram' members of such groups." Wood notes that they were also alarmed that no strong advocate for religious liberty was represented despite the "vital First Amendment concerns" that were at the heart of the debate. They warned that such a congressional hearing could become a government witch hunt and that it could "do nothing but inflame the public and obscure the delicate, complex issues which surround the activities of [religious] minority groups."[29]

Religious Solicitation Cases

Religious solicitation or fundraising by church members has also been subjected to challenges in many localities.[30] Local governments do have the power to impose limited non-discriminatory, non-burdensome regulations upon fundraisers of any religious organization.[31] However, in many instances local licensing regulations amount to unconstitutional burdens. In dozens of these situations, Unification Church members have successfully challenged and reversed these regulations. The following are a few examples:

1. In a ruling which found that Unification Church members should not be required to pay sales tax for their solicitation activities, the Michigan Court of Appeals stated:
   "The proofs put in by petitioner show that its members used the distribution of low-cost articles to facilitate the solicitation of funds. The primary purpose of this activity is to raise money for the Unification Church, which respondent concedes is a bona fide religious organization."[32]

2. The Federal District Court for the Northern District of Ohio ruled:
   "Taking into consideration the evidence in this record, it is concluded and determined that when members of the

Unification Church engage in solicitations...and when the product (candy, flowers, or religious materials) is 'made available to all those willing to listen' to a solicitor's 'witnessing on the teachings and activities of the Church, whether or not a contribution is actually made,' solicitation is a religious practice of the Church that is protected by the First Amendment."[33]

3. The Federal District Court of the Eastern District of New York wrote:
"....there is little doubt that its [Unification Church] canvassing activities must be characterized as religious for purposes of the first amendment."[34]

4. The Federal District Court of Wyoming ruled:
"There can be no doubt that 'literature evangelism' activities engaged in by the Plaintiffs Love and Martinez on behalf of the Unification Church are non-commercial in nature. Members of the Church do not receive commissions for their work. In making their door-to-door solicitations, nothing is ever sold. Contributions are requested and items may be gratuitously extended to the contributor because of his or her donation, but if a resident inquires as to the price of an item the church member explains that it is not for sale and that the item is offered to contributors only as a token of appreciation for a contribution...It is therefore the opinion of this Court that Sections 32-3 and 32-29 of the Cheyenne City Code cannot prohibit the plaintiffs Love and Martinez from engaging in their campaign of "literature evangelism," and yet remain within the confines of the constitution."[35]

The most significant solicitation case, *Larson v. Valente,*took place in the state of Minnesota, which in 1978 amended its charitable solicitation law to exclude churches which raised a majority of their funds from the public at large.[36] The amendment was enacted specifically to control solicitation by the new religious groups, including the Unification Church, and with the intention not to sweep traditional churches, particularly the Catholics, within the act.[37] The amendment was challenged by members of the Unification Church and declared unconstitutional by the district court and the Eighth Circuit Court of Appeals.

In a widely cited opinion, the United States Supreme Court upheld these lower court rulings, stating that the Minnesota statute violated the Establishment Clause of the Constitution. The high court was particularly disturbed by the fact that the legislation was drafted with the specific intention of discrimination against particular religious denominations. Justice William Brennan noted that the debates on the Minnesota Senate floor made specific reference to the goal of targeting the Unification Church. He quoted one Senator who stated: "I'm not sure why we're so hot to regulate the Moonies anyway."[38] Justice Brennan concluded that the statute "sets up precisely the sort of official denominational preference that the Framers of the First Amendment forbade."[39]

Tax Exemption

The Unification Church and its members have been subjected to discriminatory treatment by state and local government agencies on numerous other legal fronts as well. The Church has had to fight for rights that would have been granted automatically to almost any other religious organization. For example, in New York City, where the Unification movement is headquartered, the Church was initially denied property tax exemption on Church-owned buildings.

Review of this matter by the New York Court of Appeals led to a unanimous ruling which declared that the Unification Church is a *bona fide* religion. One of the most respected appellate courts in the nation, New York's highest court, stated:

> *No serious question can be raised on the record before us that the [Unification] Church has demonstrated the sincerity and the bona fides* of its assertions that in its view the political beliefs and activities of the Church and its members and the effort which they devote to fundraising and recruitment are at the core of its religious beliefs. The Tax Commission found that the Church "does in certain aspects bespeak of a religious association;" the Special Referee reported that the Church's "primary purpose is religious...."[40]

The Court added:

> *We conclude that on the record before us, as a matter of law, the primary purpose of the Church (much of whose doctrine, dogmas and teachings and a significant part of whose activities are recognized as religious) is religious and that the determination of the Tax Commission to the contrary is both arbitrary and capricious and affected by error of law.*[41]

On the basis of this key decision, tax exempt status was finally given to the Church—but only after a costly legal battle which lasted more than five years.[42]

Treatment on immigration matters has also been discriminatory. However, after many years of prejudicial treatment by the United States Immigration and Naturalization Service, the rights of the Unification Church to fair treatment were finally recognized in 1982 by the United States District Court for the District of Columbia. In granting foreign members of the Unification Church the right to enter the United States as missionaries on the same basis as members of other churches, the District Court also clearly recognized the validity and genuineness of the Unification Church: "The Unification Church, by any historical analogy, philosophical analysis or judicial precedent (indeed by INS' own criteria) must be regarded as a *bona fide* religion."[43]

Rev. Moon's Tax Case

This chapter would not be complete without at least a brief examination of Rev. Moon's 1982 tax fraud prosecution. The case is difficult to summarize in a few paragraphs due to the many issues involved and its implications for religious freedom for all denominations.

The case began in 1976 when Senator Robert Dole (R-Kan,), who had apparently accepted the anti-cult perspective on this new religious movement, urged the Internal Revenue Service to audit the Unification Church's finances. The IRS complied, beginning a five-year investigation of Unification Church records. They discovered that Rev. Moon, like most Catholic bishops and many other religious leaders, had received money from Church members who wanted to support the Church's work. To a large extent these funds came from overseas Church members who felt more confident giving money directly to Rev. Moon than to the fledgling Unification Church in the United States which was not yet organized on a national basis at that time.

Rev. Moon had duly paid taxes for the small portion of this money used for his personal expenses. The funds were primarily used to finance various activities of the Church. Over the several years that these funds were openly held in Rev. Moon's name in a Chase Manhattan Bank account, some portion was placed in interest-bearing accounts until needed. One hundred-twelve thousand dollars in interest income was earned over three years.

The government's case focused on this interest. Rev. Moon argued that he was not obliged to pay taxes on this interest because he was holding both principal and interest in trust for the Church. But in 1981 he was charged with criminal income-tax evasion. As James Manney wrote in the *National Catholic Register:*

> *On the face of it, Moon seemed to have a good case to avoid paying taxes, a better case than the average taxpayer. The reason: the law presumes that money given to a religious leader is held in trust for the Church. Nevertheless, the government threw the book at Moon. It mounted an elaborate prosecution in federal court in New York City, charging that Moon was simply a businessman, that his Church was a bogus religion, that he had conspired to defraud the government. It was bad enough that the government seemed to single out Moon for prosecution and then tried him before a hostile jury. But what really set the consitutional alarm bells ringing was the fact that the jury was allowed to pass judgment on the "religious" character of the way the money given to Moon was used. The jury decided that it served no religious purpose to let Church contributions sit in an interest-bearing bank account until the money was needed. Thus Moon was guilty as charged. In essence, a New York jury defined "religion."*[44]

Outcry by Religious Community

The outcry in support of Rev. Moon on the part of the religious community, not to mention civil liberties organizations, has rarely been seen in United States legal history. More than forty organizations and individuals representing an estimated 125 million Americans filed *amicus curiae* (friend of the court) briefs in support of Reverend Moon's petition for *certiorari* to the United States Supreme Court. They included religious leaders from both ends of the American political spectrum such as the Rev. Jerry Falwell of the Moral Majority and the Rev. Joseph Lowery of the Southern Christian Leadership Conference. Also included were such national religious organizations as the National Council of Churches, the National Association of Evangelicals, the United Presbyterian Church, the American Baptist Churches, the African Methodist Episcopal Church, and the Church of Jesus Christ of Latter-day Saints (Mormons). In addition, briefs were filed by the Christian Legal Society, the American Civil Liberties Union, the Catholic League for Religious and Civil Rights and others.

In the words of *Washington Post* columnist Colman McCarthy, "This is a Noah's ark of views and styles. Everyone is on board, not to express faith in Moon but to perform the good works of protecting his right to express his Unification beliefs. If his church is under unfair attack this time, someone else's may be next time."[45]

One *amicus* brief filed by a coalition of major religious organizations, including the National Council of Churches, *et al,* stated that the Second Circuit opinion upheld "a grave subversion of religious liberty and due proces—one that is cause for deep alarm."[46] They were particularly concerned that, in light of past decisions interpreting the First Amendment Clauses, the lower court had upheld a verdict which had not fully taken into account various religious notions and explanations offered by Rev. Moon to explain his actions. These major religious organizations pointed out that this issue "is critical to followers of *all* faiths." Furthermore, the *amici* brief argued:

> *From the tax-exempt status of a church parking lot, to the validity of an incorporated church association's assertion of power to direct the actions of a church corporation, little of what even modern-day mainstream churches routinely do would survive intact if squeezed through a religion-extracting filter in flat disregard to the First Amendment.*[47]

The Catholic League for Religious and Civil Rights further pointed out that though the jury determined that certain property was owned personally by Rev. Moon and used for his benefit rather than for religious purposes, "This determination was made with few clear standards, certainly was not in deference to the Church's position, and was not an application of any clearly recognized neutral principles of law."[48]

It was evident that the Catholic League was especially fearful of any possible extension of such governmental action to other groups. The Catholic League argued that other religious groups are now in danger as a result of the *Moon* decision, especially the Roman Catholic Church. As stated earlier, many Roman Catholic religious leaders and bishops hold church property in their own names "consistent with the canon law premise that, '[i]n all juridical transactions of the diocese, the diocesan Bishop acts in the person of the diocese.'"[49] Therefore, the Catholic League logically determined that its Catholic bishops potentially face the same sort of federal tax prosecution imposed against Rev. Moon.

The American Civil Liberties Union (ACLU), along with other civil rights organizations such as the Southern Christian Leadership Conference, expressed profound concern that Rev. Moon was forced to stand trial before a jury, despite clear evidence that public hostility towards him was so deep-seated that only a bench trial would have provided a fair trial. In an *amicus curiae* brief, the ACLU stated: "The government's insistence on a jury when both the defendant and the judge believed that a bench trial would be fairer simply reinforced public suspicion that Rev. Moon was the target of religious persecution."[50]

The final upshot of the case was that the Supreme Court refused to hear the case and Rev. Moon served thirteen months in a federal correctional institution, from July 20, 1984 to August 20, 1985. This was an extremely painful period for Rev. Moon, his family and for the entire movement. Nevertheless, it is believed by many people that Rev. Moon may have gained far more than he lost from this difficult experience. In the eyes of many individuals, particularly clergymen, Rev. Moon is a victim of religious persecution. Because of his willingness to go this course voluntarily,[51] without complaint, he is now seen as a leading champion and spokesman for religious freedom.

Rev. Moon's struggle also had a significant impact in galvanizing public concern for the religious liberty of all people. Numerous rallies were held across the United States and elsewhere during 1984, drawing attention to the little known fact that churches of all types are being subjected to the greatest legal assault in America's history.[52]

One of the many individuals who supported Rev. Moon's appeal was U.S. Senator Orrin Hatch, Chairman of the Senate Subcommittee on the Constitution. Through the investigation conducted into Rev. Moon's case by his Senate Subcommittee, he was able to obtain access to secret documents which the U.S. Department of Justice had previously refused to disclose. His extensive investigation led him to the conclusion that "injustice rather than justice has been served" by this prosecution. Senator Hatch stated:

* *The three Justice Department attorneys who intially undertook an independent review of a possible criminal action against Rev.Moon unanimously agreed, independently of each other, that there was no case.*

* *According to the Justice Department's review, Rev. Moon's tax liability, even if the government's case could be proved, was a mere $7,300 for a three-year period [or roughly $2,433 per year]. I have been advised that the Justice Department's own guidelines state that criminal tax cases will not be brought if the alleged tax deficiency is less than $2,500 per year.*

* *Despite the career attorneys' recommendations not to prosecute, and no evidence of any kind to establish that even a single cent of the money in dispute was given to Rev. Moon personally, and not to his church, the Justice Department was nevertheless persuaded to seek an indictment by a zealous assistant U.S. Attorney in the Southern District of New York, who built a case entirely on supposition and innuendo.*

* *At the trial, the judge eliminated any mention of religion. In doing so, he permitted the jury to substitute its own views for those of the Unification Church on crucial issues dealing with what constitutes a religious purpose and how money could be spent within the Unification Church.*

* *Despite how people may feel about his religious beliefs, he [Rev. Moon] is universally recognized as a humanitarian and is dedicated to a serious fight against communism and in favor of democratic ideals. He constantly praises America and what she stands for, even after his trial.*

* *It is well documented that since coming to the United States, [the Unification movement] has spent large sums of money in various activities including, for example, ownership of* The Washington Times, *in which, by conservative estimate, the financial losses have exceeded $100 million over the past three years. It simply makes no sense whatsoever to expect that a man who has managerial control over such large sums of money would intentionally conspire to avoid a few thousand dollars in income taxes.*[53]

As this brief survey indicates, the Unification Church has established a remarkably successful record in fighting its legal battles. In the process, it has added a great deal to the cause of religious liberty for everyone.

Constitutional expert Jeremiah Gutman asserts that the Unification Church is performing the kind of service in First Amendment litigation that has in the past been performed by other churches which have been the victims of religious persecution. He suggests that First Amendment law tends to move forward when an unpopular religion is attacked and then vindicated. And, he adds, the Unification Church has been vindicated on every First Amendmant issue it has faced.[54]

References

1. See Robert T. Haney, *A Christian America: Protestant hopes and historical realities* (New York: Oxford University Press, 1971) 30; Sydney E. Ahlstrom, *A Religious History of the American People* (New Haven: Yale University Press, 1972) 1-11; and Alfred J. Sciarrino, "'Free Exercise' Footsteps in the Defamation Forest: Are 'New Religions' Lost?", *The American Journal of Trial Advocacy*, Vol. 7, 1984, 59-60.

2. Leo Pfeffer, *Church, State and Religious Freedom*, 1967, 645-50.

3. *Molko and Leal v. HSA*, 179 Cal. App. 3d 450, 1986. At this writing, this case is on appeal to the California Supreme Court.

4. Ibid., 470.

5. See trial court opinion, *Molko and Leal v. HSA*, Superior Court of San Francisco, No. 769529, Oct. 20, 1983, 9-10.

6. Ibid.

7. Ibid. See also Court of Appeal opinion, 179 Cal. App. 3d 450, 467, n. 9.

8. *Molko*, 179 Cal. App. 3d 450, 467, 470.

9. *United States v. Ballard*, 322 U.S. 78, 86-87, 1944.

10. *Molko*, 179 Cal. App. 3d 450, 474.

11. Ibid.

12. Ibid. Some of the other legal victories on this issue include *Lewis v. HSA-UWC*, 589 F. Supp. 10, D. MA, 1983; *Schuppin v. Unification Church*, 435 F. Sup. 603, D. VT, 1977; *Turner v. Unification Church*, 473 F. Supp 367, D. RI, 1978. See also *Katz v. Superior Court*, infra.

13. *Katz v. Superior Court,* 73 Cal. App. 3d 952, 1977.

14. Le Moult, supra, 617.

15. *Katz,* supra, 988-89. The appeals court stressed the tradition of religious liberty in America. The court quoted extensively from the classic United States Supreme Court statement on religious liberty in *United States v. Ballard: "Many take their gospel from the New Testament. But it would hardly be supposed that they could be tried before a jury charged with the duty of determining whether those teachings contained false representations. The miracles of the New Testament, the Divinity of Christ, life after death, the power of prayer are deep in the religious convictions of many. If one could be sent to jail because a jury in a hostile environment found those teachings false, little indeed would be left of religious freedom. The Fathers of the Constitution were not unaware of the varied and extreme views of religious sects, of the violence of disagreement among them and of the lack of any one religious creed on which all men would agree. They fashioned a charter of government which envisaged the widest possible toleration of conflicting views. Man's relation to his God was made no concern of the state. He was granted the right to worship as he pleased and to answer to no man for the verity of his religious views. The religious views espoused by respondents might seem incredible, if not preposterous, to most people. But if those doctrines are subject to trial before a jury charged with finding their truth or falsity, then the same can be done with the religious beliefs of any sect. When the triers of fact undertake that task, they enter a forbidden domain." Katz,* 986, quoting *U.S. v. Ballard,* 322 U.S. 78, 1944.

16. *Meroni v. Holy Spirit Association,* Westchester County No. 3811/80, App. Div. (2nd Dept.) Supreme Court of New York, Sept. 2, 1986.

17. Ibid., 6.

18. Ibid., 7.

19. 764 F. 2d 122, 2d Cir. 1985.

19*. Thomas Robbins, "'Uncivil Religions' and Religious Deprogramming," *Thought, Fordham University Quarterly,* Vol. LXI, June 1986, 283. Robbins laments that this case "shows how easily the question of whether a convert's rights were violated by the use of physical force can be redefined (arguably swept under the rug) so that the court's attention is redirected to the doctrines and practices of the disfavored sect." Ibid.

20. Ibid., 130-131. quoting *Taylor v. Gilmartin,* 686 F. 2d 1346, 1357, 1982.

21. Ibid., 131. Other legal victories on this issue include *Ward v. Connor,* 657 F. 2d 45, 4th Cir., 1981, *cert denied,* 102 S. Ct. 1253, 1982; *Rankin v. Howard,* 633 F. 2d 844, 9th Cir., 1980; *Cooper v. Molko,* 512 F. Supp. 563, ND Cal., 1981.

22. James E. Wood, Jr., "New Religions and the First Amendment," *Journal of Church and State,* Vol. 24, 1982, 457-459.

23. In a response to Mr. Fraser's harassment, Dr. Bo Hi Pak, Special Assistant to Rev. Moon published a statement which concluded with a definition of "witch-hunt," as found in the *Living Webster Encyclopedia Dictionary of the English Language:* "A public investigation ostensibly conducted to detect subversion, used as a forum for arbitrary accusations by the investigators against unpopular or powerless individuals in order to acquire a reputation for vigilant patriotism." Dr. Pak added: "I pray to God that this will not be the case with Rep. Donald M. Fraser's Subcommittee." *Day of Hope III* (Tarrytown, NY: IOWC, 1981) 1227.

24. Bromley and Shupe wrote: "In the end, after a long string of testimonies, subpoenaed records and documents, and discrediting facts had been amassed, little beyond continuing to monitor Moon's various organizations could be done officially. Despite talk of the "numerous violations" revealed by the [Fraser] committee, none seemed serious and certainly none moved any federal

agency to prosecute or investigate the UM [Unification movement] further." Bromley & Shupe, *New Vigilantes,* supra, 189.

25. Wood, supra, 457.

26. *Southern California Law Review,* Vol. 51, 1977,1.

27. Hearings, Vermont Senate Comm. for the Investigation of Alleged, Deceptive, Fraudulent and Criminal Practices of Various Organizations in the State, Aug. 18, 1976; Sept. 22, 1976.

28. Frank Flinn, "Criminalizing Conversion," supra.

29. Wood, supra, 459.

30. Sciarrino, supra, 59.

31. See, for example, *Heffron v. ISKCON,* 452 U.S. 640, 1981; Sciarrino, supra, 324-325.

32. *HSA-UWC v. Michigan Dept. of Treasury,* 313 MI App. 743, 754, 1984.

33. *McMurdie v. Doutt,* 468 F. Supp. 766, 772, N.D. Ohio, 1979.

34. *Troyer v. Town of Babylon,* 483 F. Supp. 1135, 1137, E.D. NY, 1980.

35. *Love v. Mayor, City of Cheyenne,* 448 F. Supp. 128, 130, 131, 133, D. WY, 1978.

36. Minn. Stat. S 309.515 (1)(b), 1980.

37. *Compare* Remarks of Senator Deitrich, Hearing before Minn. Sen. Subcomm. on Judicial Admin., Mar. 7, 1978, (voice tape recording) *with* Remarks of Special Assistant Attorney General Luzzie, Hearing on Minn. House Comm. on Commerce and Econ. Dev., Jan. 24, 1978, (voice tape recording).

38. *Larson v. Valente,* 456 U.S. 228, 255, 1982.

39. Ibid.

40. *Holy Spirit Association for the Unification of World Christianity v. Tax Commission of the City of New York,* 55, NY 2d 512, 526, 1982.

41. Ibid., 528.

42. Since this important decision, the City of New York has fully accepted the exempt status of the Unification Church. A March 20, 1986 letter from the Deputy Commisioner for Legal Affairs stated: "By letter dated November 20, 1963,the organization was granted exemption from federal income tax under section 501 (c)(3) of the Internal Revenue Code, which is comparable to the vault charge exemption provision quoted above. The federal exemption was recently confirmed by the District Director of the Internal Revenue Service, by letter dated November 27, 1985. In addition, in a National Office Technical Advice Memorandum attached to the District Director's letter, the National Office of the Internal Revenue Service specifically found that there was no basis to revoke the organization's exemption either for "political activities" or "inurement." Moveover, in connection with the organization's application for exemption from real property taxes, the Court of Appeals held that HSA-UWC is an organization "organized and operated exclusively for religious...purposes..." Based on the foregoing, we conclude that HSA-UWC is entitled to exemption from the City's annual vault charge."

43. *Unification Church v. Immigration and Naturalization Service,* 547 F. Supp. 623, 628, 1982.

44. "More Than Moon Is At Stake Here," *National Catholic Register,* Los Angeles, California, June 17, 1984.

45. The Real Issue in the Case of Rev. Moon," *The Washington Post,* Washington, DC, Feb. 5, 1984.

46. Brief for the National Council of Churches *et al,* in support of petition for *certiorari* to the United States Supreme Court in *United States v. Sun Myung Moon,* 5.

47. Ibid., 18.

48. Brief for the Catholic League for Religious and Civil Rights, in support of petition for *certiorari* to the United States Supreme Court in *United States v. Sun Myung Moon,* 3.

49. Ibid., 5, quoting Canon 393 of *The Code of Canon Law,* 1983.

50. Brief for the American Civil Liberties Union, in support of petition for *certiorari* to the United States Supreme Court in *United States v. Sun Myung Moon,* 12.

51. Rev. Moon returned voluntarily from Korea to face the indictment despite the fact that the United States has no extradition treaty with South Korea.

52. See, for example, "Moon jailing unifies government foes," *Press Herald,* (Portland, Maine), Aug. 11, 1984; "Black ministers, rightist rally behind Rev. Moon," *San Francisco Examiner,* (San Francisco, California), Aug. 31, 1984; "Moon's imprisonment condemned by U.S. churches," *Pittsburgh Post-Gazette,* (Pittsburgh, Pennsylvania), Aug. 10, 1984; "Rally raps government 'attacks' on churches," *St. Paul Dispatch,* (St. Paul, Minnesota), Aug. 28, 1984.

53. "Moon Victim of Government Conspiracy," *Oakland Post,* (Oakland, California), July 3, 1985. Legal commentator Alfred J. Sciarrino of the New York State Attorney General's Office offers a detailed overview in "United States v. Sun Myung Moon: Precedent for Tax Fraud Prosecution of Local Pastors?" *Southern Illinois University Law Journal,* 1984, 237. He concludes: "no recent case raises as many important issues as this action, or poses such an immediate threat to religious liberty." Ibid., 281.

54. Jeremiah S. Gutman, interview with author, September 9, 1986. The tax case against Rev. Moon is not included here because it was not a prosecution against the Unification Church.

Chapter 9

SOME REMAINING ISSUES

The preceding chapters deal with some of the major causes of the early fear and hysteria surrounding new religions. As they have grown and become more fully understood, they have seen the apprehension and hostility begin to dissipate. Nevertheless, there are a number of specific misconceptions that have continued to linger. This chapter will clarify some of the major ones in regard to the Unification Church.

1. *What attracts People?*

Given all of the controversy surrounding the Unification Church over the years, some people may wonder what it is that attracts people to the movement. To the uninformed, it has been alleged that members of this group are "zombies" totally manipulated by a Korean industrialist. It has been charged that the Unification Church is not a genuine religion at all but simply a huge business empire designed to satisfy the self-aggrandizing and power-hungry desires of Sun Myung Moon.

In reality, however, Unificationists are motivated by an intense religious faith grounded in a comprehensive set of beliefs. It is not the purpose of this book to teach Unification theology, but it is useful to give a brief overview in order to respond to the charges that have been made.[1]

Unification theology states that human beings are created in God's image as His children and that love is the power that binds each person to God and to others. There is a tremendous emphasis on the centrality of love as the motivating force behind God's creation of the universe, and on the absolute requirement of God's love in resolving the massive problems in the world.

Of particular importance is the belief in a *living* God who is intimately aware of each and every one of His children. This stems from the belief that the purpose, the motivating force behind the creation of the universe, was God's desire for an object to love, for someone to respond to His love. If human beings are created in the image of God, then our desire for someone to love must be a reflection of God's deep longing for a most profound and intimate relationship with His precious sons and daughters. It is for this reason that God is so excruciatingly aware of mankind's suffering and struggle and also why God implores His children to care for one another and work urgently to end the suffering of their brothers and sisters. This understanding is the basis for Unification belief in the family of humankind.

On the basis of a profound belief that all human beings are brothers and sisters under the common parenthood of God, Unificationists believe that humankind can begin to resolve the tremendous historical breakdown among families, races, religions and nationalities. The love that forms the core of this human family originates within the God-centered family. The essence of the God-centered family involves first and foremost developing a mature relationship of love with God. As people achieve this level of maturity, they are able to fulfill what Jesus described as the two great commandments:

> *You shall love the Lord your God with all your heart, and with all your soul, and with all your mind. This is the great and first commandment. And a second is like it, You shall love your neighbor as yourself. On these two commandments depend all the law and the prophets.*[2]

On this foundation, a man and a woman are ready to enter into a relationship of conjugal love as husband and wife. They are then capable of providing the kind of unconditional love necessary to build the wholesome, stable families that should constitute the building blocks for an ideal society.

Unificationists interpret the course of human history as a long and painful struggle, whereby God has been working tirelessly to fulfill His ideal of the Kingdom of Heaven on earth. They feel that we are living today in a very crucial period in human history, a time when a great deal can be accomplished towards establishing God's eternal ideal on the earth. It is their conviction that they can contribute in a significant way towards building God's kingdom, and they strongly believe that Rev. Moon is fulfilling a prophetic role for this age, coming as an important messenger from God.

2. *Who is Reverend Moon?*

Much controversy has centered on the spiritual leader and founder of the Unification Church, Rev. Sun Myung Moon. He was born in 1920 to a deeply religious family in what is now North Korea. While praying on a Korean hillside on

Easter morning in 1936, Rev. Moon had an experience with Jesus Christ, who asked him to help complete the task of building the Kingdom of Heaven on earth. Theologian Richard Quebedeaux writes: "For the next nine years Moon studied the Bible, prayed intensely, and like the early Christian hermits in the desert, had spiritual battles with the cosmic forces of evil. In course of time he discovered the (Divine) Principle, the basis of the Unification Church's inspired interpretation of the Bible."[3]

In 1946, while multitudes of his fellow countrymen fled south, he felt called by God to journey north to preach the Gospel in North Korea, which had recently become communist. Teaching his revelation, he quickly attracted a large following. The communist authorities, however, saw Rev. Moon and his message as a threat and they arrested him without warning. He was taken to the Dae Dong Police Department and mercilessly tortured and beaten until he was believed dead. The guards then threw his body into a snowbank outside the prison yard. He was found there later by members of his congregation, who held little hope for his survival. He did survive, however, supported by the prayers and attention of his followers.

Despite the intense persecution, Rev. Moon continued his teaching of the Bible and vigorous propagation of God's message. As a result, he was again arrested in 1948 and charged with "spreading lies among the people" and sentenced to five years in a labor camp near Hungnam, North Korea. Hungnam was literally a death camp where the prisoners were systematically starved and worked to death. Their work consisted of filling hundred-pound bags with caustic fertilizer and loading them onto railroad cars. The lime from the fertilizer ate away the skin and flesh of their hands until the bones showed. Most prisoners, tormented beyond human physical limitations, endured little more than a few months of this slow death. Through a profound faith in God, Rev. Moon survived there for almost three years. In October 1950, he was liberated by the United Nations forces sent to defend South Korea.[3*]

Shortly after his liberation, Rev. Moon walked hundreds of miles to the south along with thousands of other refugees, much of the way carrying one of his injured disciples. He settled in Pusan and there built his first "church" — a tiny mud hut constructed from cardboard U.S. Army ration boxes

— on a hillside overlooking the city. In 1954 he officially founded the Holy Spirit Association for the Unification of World Christianity, which has become commonly known as the Unification Church. He came to America in late 1971 to begin an evangelical ministry, traveling to each of the fifty states to preach a religious reawakening.

3. *What does the Church do for the World?*

In his preaching, Rev. Moon has placed particular focus on what he calls "three major headaches of God:" the conflict and disunity among the world's religions, the increasing immorality in society and the expansion of atheistic communism. To alleviate these problems, he has urged his followers to undertake a vast array of projects. One of the most prominent of these has been the effort to bring together theologians and clergy from all religious faiths to engage in dialogue and cooperation.[4] The International Religious Foundation (IRF), for instance, recently sponsored the Assembly of the World's Religions, bringing together more than 600 religious leaders, scholars, and spiritualists from around the world (Nov. 15—21, 1985). For many years, IRF has also sponsored a conference called "God: The Contemporary Discussion" which has brought together hundreds of theologians from a broad range of religious faiths to share their beliefs and experiences of God.[5]

Unificationists place a great deal of importance on this dialogue as do other leading ecumenical theologians such as Hans Kung. Father Kung expresses his views on this subject as follows: "Only if we seek to understand others' faith can we really understand our own; its strengths and weaknesses, its constants and variables." Kung adds: " Only if we seek to understand others' faith can we discover that common ground which, despite all differences, can become the basis for a peaceful life in this world together."[6]

The ecumenical sensibility of the Unification Movement is perhaps nowhere better expressed than at the Church's "Unificaton Theological Seminary" in Barrytown, New York. The faculty of this seminary is noted for the fact that it includes professors from nearly every major religious faith, from Catholic to Jew and Reformed Church to Islam and Hindu.[7] In recent years, the ecumenical outreach has had a special focus on bringing together members of the Christian clergy to discuss mutual concerns, particularly in regard to the breakdown of morality, the growing use of drugs and the increasing disintegration of the famiy unit.

The concept of reviving a moral world view has also been at the core of the annual International Conference on the Unity of the Sciences (ICUS) sponsored by the International Cultural Foundation (ICF) since 1972. Unificationists believe that making the world a better place cannot be achieved by religion alone. It can only be done in conjunction with all disciplines, particularly by the unity of science and religion, which has been the focus of the ICUS Conferences.

The need for cooperation among all facets of society to build a better world has also led Unificationists to become actively involved in a broad range of activities from science and academics to media and business. They are also involved in supporting various charitable and relief projects such as the International Relief Friendship Foundation (IRFF), Project Volunteer (PV) and International Christians for Unity and Social Action (ICUSA) which seek to provide food, medical supplies and other services to the needy in the United States and around the world.

In regard to the third major "headache" of God, Rev. Moon has founded CAUSA as a non-denominational educational foundation to explain communism from a religious point of view. More specifically, the CAUSA Lecture Program offers a detailed critique of Marxist/Leninist ideology both in theory and in practice as well as a counterproposal referred to as "Godism."[8]

There are too many projects to name in this short summary.[9] Suffice it to say that the Unification Church strongly believes in the principle: "practice what you preach." Many people have joined because they have felt that they are part of a concrete and practical effort to make a better world, that they are not just paying "lip-service" to their beliefs and their ideals but are actually doing something.

4. *Why the Emphasis on Anti-Communism?*

The strong commitment of the Unification Church to exposing the evils of communism as espoused by the

Marxist/Leninist ideology has often been misunderstood and has led to accusations of political intentions. To some, there is a sense that Unification Church members seek a military solution to this problem and that there is a tendency to be "reactionary" conservatives. The reality is that many Church members support a contemporary liberal stand on issues such as social justice and racial equality, but often take a more conservative stance when it comes to protecting traditional religious values, particularly the ultimate value of religious freedom denied both in theory and in practice by Marxist/Leninists. The great civil rights leader Martin Luther King, Jr. similarly condemned communism:

> *First, Communism is based on a materialistic and humanistic view of life and history. According to Communist theory, matter, not mind or spirit, speaks the last word in the universe. Such a philosophy is avowedly secularistic and atheistic....*
>
> *Second, Communism is based on ethical relativism and accepts no stable moral absolutes. Right and wrong are relative to the most expedient methods for dealing with class war. Communism exploits the dreadful philosophy that the end justifies the means. It enunciates movingly the theory of a classless society, but alas! its methods for achieving this noble end are all too often ignoble. Lying, violence, murder, and torture are considered to be justifiable means to achieve the millennial end. Is this an unfair indictment? Listen to the words of Lenin, the real tactician of Communist theory: "We must be ready to employ trickery, deceit, lawbreaking, withholding and concealing truth." Modern history has known many tortuous nights and horror-filled days because his followers have taken this statement seriously.*[10]

It is because of their overriding commitment to the freedom and well-being of all people that Unificationists have great concern about the global advancement of Marxist/Leninism. For this reason, most members support a strong national defense but only insofar as it is necessary to protect freedom. There is an overriding belief that freedom to choose one's religion and one's way of life are inalienable rights which come directly from the Creator. These rights have been held as supreme for generations, and people have historically been willing to give their lives to defend and preserve these freedoms. The present should be no exception.

The essence of Rev. Moon's teaching is that ultimately only love can resolve human problems and, therefore, military might and war will never resolve the historical tragedy of the human condition. Violence only breeds further violence. As he and many others have said, the cycle of hate has to end somewhere, and that is only possible through a heart of compassion, forgiveness and love.

5. *Why the Large Weddings?*

The large weddings have drawn much fire and ridicule from critics of the Unification Church, particularly the practice of "arranged" marriages. To some in Western society, it is difficult to comprehend how intelligent young men and women would be willing to allow an Oriental man to suggest their marriage partner. To give some perspective to the issue, it is important to consider that many young men and women in today's society already hold little confidence in the institution of marriage because there has been so much family breakdown. The fact that Unification Church members are able to marry another person who shares the same hopes, dreams and vision for the future gives them much greater confidence that their families can be successful. It is for this reason that most members ask Rev. Moon to suggest someone to be their spouse.

Members believe that God will guide Rev. Moon to suggest the partner who best complements their character and who will assist them in their spiritual growth. They believe that the basis for his suggestions is far more reliable from a spiritual perspective than the computer-dating method or the pick-up at the local bar or disco that many people in Western society use. Besides, anyone who has seen "Fiddler on the Roof" or studied history or present-day world cultures knows that this practice of match-making is far from unique to the Unification Church. In fact, arranged marriages in the Unification Church and elsewhere produce a proportion of successful marriages *much* higher than that of self-arranged marriages in the United States today.

After Rev. Moon makes his recommendation to a Unification couple, they meet together to discuss whether they are prepared to accept his suggestion. In many cases, they have known each other for some years. In other cases they may never have met, so this initial meeting is special and highly significant. Because of a great trust in Rev. Moon's judgment and also a trust that this other person is dedicated to the same principles and ideals, many couples accept his suggestion. Nevertheless, there are other instances where the two individuals decide not to accept. In these cases, they usually ask him to suggest someone else. Church members may also express a preference for a particular person and invite his blessing.

Following the engagement ceremony, there is usually a period of months and sometimes two or three years before the couples are actually married. It is during this time that the couples begin to build their relationship and prepare for their future life together. This is also when romance begins. Rev. Moon teaches that the marriage relationship is meant to be the place where God's love dwells at the center of a cosmic, romantic love between husband and wife.

Catholic sociologist Joseph Fichter writes that for Unification Church members marriage is a serious, holy and obligatory "sacrament" for which lengthy preparation is required. He points out that although the concept of "arranged" marriage is alien to young Americans, "it has been an accepted pattern for most of humanity for most of human history." He adds:

> *Preoccupation with the dating game, the hazards of flirty infatuation...are avoided in the custom of arranged marriages. The attraction to each other is spiritually motivated and spiritually sustained. They are putting God's will, as expressed to them by their religious leader, before their own. As in everything else they do, the primary motive in preparing for marriage is to follow the will of God."*[11]

The large wedding ceremonies are highly significant in the Unification tradition. They represent the public pledge that each person dedicates his or her life to their spouse before God.

Even more importantly, the ceremony represents the pledge of all of the couples to the service of God and all of mankind, hence the motto of the 1982 Madison Square Garden Wedding: "World Peace Through Ideal Families." The large weddings that most people identify with the Unification Church are ceremonies of public dedication to God by a large group of couples who offer themselves as representatives of the world.[12]

James H. Grace, chairman of the Philosophy and Religion Department at Glassboro College, in his book *Sex and Marriage in the Unification Movement, A Sociological Study,* offers an outsider's perspective following an exhaustive study "carried out according to the most rigorous scientific procedures."[13] He says that he is personally convinced that America—especially the religious institutions—could learn something very important about marriage from a careful and candid consideration of the Unification ideal. He calls this a lesson "which points to a way out of our present marital quandry."[14]

Grace suggests that the ideal for marriage in the Unification Church could not only restore a sense of social responsibility to the Christian home, but it could also help to relieve the "pressure cooker" atmosphere that exists in many marriage relationships today. Grace says that this is because spouses expect too much "ego-fulfillment" from each other which spawns pressures and expectations that inhibit both freedom and intimacy in the marriage. It leads the couple "to focus exclusively on the impossible task of meeting all or most of each others' needs" rather than having a shared commitment to the world, as in Unification Church marriages which see their relationship as destined by God to serve the human community.[15] Grace concludes:

> *The Unification ideal for marriage suggests that we do not have to follow the way of our acquisitive society and its emphasis on possessions as the key to happiness. The family that puts its responsibility to the world community above wealth and possessions will, I believe, find that the love which it shares with others will also glow brightly in the home.*[16]

6. Does the Church Break up Families?

One of the central areas of controversy has been the allegation that the Unification Church breaks up families. However, the reality is that this is absolutely *not* a part of the teaching of the Unification Church,[17] nor is it the reality for the vast majority of members. As Father Fichter reports from his extensive contact with Unification Church members, the great majority maintain good relations with their parents and family.[18]

There have been numerous well-publicized incidents of breakdown between Unification Church members and their families, but these are the exception. Most can be understood in the context of the traditional or typical family misunderstanding (as explained earlier) when an offspring or sibling joins a new religious movement. Fichter compares this to similar charges that have been made "about Catholic religious orders that lured a daughter to the convent or a son to the seminary." As Father Fichter remarks, "God's call must be obeyed even if parents are in opposition."[19]

It is also worth noting that this is a phenomenon that occurs quite infrequently now that the movement has become more established, more mature and its members are more settled and are raising families of their own. In many ways, the Unification movement has changed dramatically since its early pioneer days. Now that so many members are married and raising families, the majority no longer live in a communal lifestyle. Thus the accusation of locked doors, gates and guards to prevent members from escaping has become even more unreal and ridiculous. The idea of escaping from one's own wife and children doesn't make any sense.

The general feeling among parents of Unification Church members varies from those who have themselves converted to the Church to those who still hold a great many reservations and sometimes anger about their offspring's involvement. The majority are supportive or at least sympathetic because they have come to recognize that the Church has helped their sons and daughters become sincere, hardworking, God-centered individuals. The following are a few examples of reactions by parents. One mother from Florida states:

> *I was skeptical about the Unification Church until I had the opportunity to visit it recently. I have never seen a group of young people with higher morals or more dedicated to improving mankind. The opportunity of seeing so much consideration and love for one's fellow man is almost unheard of today. I am ashamed to say that so many of our so-called society of good church-goers do not begin to live the real Christian life like this group of dedicated young people do. The change in our son has made us very happy."*[20]

Another mother from California took time to investigate the church and concludes:

> *About six years ago my daughter decided to become a member. As a mother, naturally I was quite concerned in the beginning. Rather than sit around at home and worry, I decided to learn all about it. I went to the Church centers and listened to many lectures, attended services and participated in the many activities of the Church. I did not depend on hearsay, rumors or news media for my informaion. I studied the books and pamphlets published by the Unification Church. The Church teaches the members to honor and respect their parents and grandparents and relatives....*[21]

Another parent says that she had seen many of the bad press reports and the "shocking" headlines. Instead of jumping to conclusions, she describes her reaction as thinking "that can't really be Jenny's church—it doesn't sound like it at all." Her next step was to visit the local church center where she was impressed with all of the members she met. Over the years she attended numerous church events where she saw the kind of life church members led, "how hard they worked and how they gave up so much and dedicated their lives to working for God."[22]

As can be seen from the foregoing examples, the relationships between Unificationists and their families often deepen as a result of their involvement with the Church. Furthermore, the Unification movement has matured. It is not nearly as unknown or mistrusted as during the 1970s and the lifestyle is not as intense and strictly disciplined as it appeared in earlier days. The lifestyle that seemed to pose a threat to established society during the early days has, to a large extent, given way to the more traditional and accepted lifestyle of married couples raising children.[23]

7. *Why so much Real Estate?*

Another area of controversy has been the oft-repeated claim that Rev. Moon or the Unification Church owns vast amounts of real estate in the United States. First of all, Rev. Moon does not own any real estate in the United States. The Unification Church of America (the corporate name is the Holy Spirit Association for the Unification of World Christianity) does own various properties, but to allege that they are "vast" holdings is inaccurate.

The Unification Church owns at least one piece of property in most of the fifty states. These properties are usually modest homes that have been converted into church centers. In addition, the Church owns several retreat centers in various parts of the country. Excluding the larger properties in the New York City area a rough estimate of the value of U.S. properties would be $15-20 million (based on purchase price).

The Church owns its most substantial properties in the New York area. By far the largest is the former New Yorker Hotel which now serves as the World Mission Center for the church's activities worldwide, including foreign mission work in more than one hundred-thirty countries. It also serves as the headquarters for numerous organizations founded by Rev. Moon and as a residence for several hundred missionary members and their families. It was purchased for $5.6 million in 1976. The Manhattan Center, which adjoins the World Mission Center and is used for cultural activities, was purchased for $3 million in 1976. The National Headquarters building, which serves as headquarters for Church activities in the United States and in New York City, and houses approximately one hundred missionaries, was purchased for $1.2 million in 1975.

The Church owns a number of small centers in the vicinity of New York City. In Westchester County, New York the Church owns a number of homes and parcels of land as well as several larger properties which are used to house Church members and to serve as educational and conference centers for the worldwide membership of the Church.

Without going into detail, there is the Unification Theological Seminary at Barrytown, as well as retreat facilities at Mt. Kisco and Accord, New York. The value of the New York area properties is in the neighborhood of $20-25 million (based on purchase price).

This brings the total for U.S. properties to approximately $35-45 million. To a private individual, this may sound like a great deal, but when one considers that these properties are used for the operation of an active religious ministry throughout the United States and throughout the world, they are miniscule. For the sake of comparison, the book *The Religious Empire* by Martin Larson and Stanley Lowell, estimates that the Roman Catholic Archdiocese of Baltimore *alone* owns property worth nearly $200 million (based on 1974 figures).[24] This is five times the holdings of the Unification Church in all of the United States.

Larson, who has authored numerous books on this issue, and Lowell, who is a clergyman, author and former editor of *Church and State* magazine, estimate that in 1973 the United Methodist Church owned tax exempt property valued at more than $7 billion.[25] This amount comes to 175 times the value of real estate owned by the Unification Church in the United States.

8. Why Endure the Persecution?

The tremendous controversy that has surrounded the Church raises the question as to why Unification Church members would be willing to endure the kind of abuse and persecution to which they have been subjected. However, as one could observe from the Catholic experience, the Mormon experience, the experience of the Jehovah's Witnesses, or many others, the fact that the Unification Church has received a great deal of persecution has actually given members greater motivation. It has energized the movement. The challenge posed by persecution can serve to strengthen one's faith because it forces adherents to constantly test, re-evaluate and reconfirm their beliefs in order to carry on.[26] The record of history is a testimony to the fact that the materialistic world often rejects the prophet sent by God in a given age and that initially it is often just a small group of disciples who are able to grasp the message and eventually spread that message to the larger world. Unification Church members believe they are following in that tradition.

Such a test of faith was especially real to members of the Unification Church in England following the unsuccessful libel suit aginst the *Daily Mail* in 1981. Mike Breen, who is now a free-lance foreign correspondent, wrote a letter to the editor of the *Daily Mail* at that time. He advised the newspaper that its crusade against the Church had made members stronger and that many supporters had decided to speak out publicly in support of the Unification Church because of the persecution. He also wrote that Rev. Moon had suffered unspeakable persecution all his life:

> *It is from his example that we learn to endure persecution. He teaches us, "Never condemn those who persecute you, pray for them." He also teaches us, "Do not think of yourselves, but think rather of God. He has suffered more than anyone." In your book that is probably brainwashng....Therefore, to you, Rev. Moon must be evil and self-centered, exploiting the young idealist/brainwashees. Actually, we get our idealistic zeal from Rev. Moon; it is not something he exploits.*
>
> *There is an old Indian saying—"If you want to understand a man, you must walk a mile in his moccasins." You do not understand us. You would not dream of walking a mile in our moccasins. You just condemn us.*
>
> *As Rev. Moon has taught us, we are praying for you and your newspaper. We are praying that it may use its tremendous influence to change this country for the good and bring it back to God. That is our simple prayer.*[27]

Despite the fact that persecution helped to energize the movement, it also served as a tremendous challenge to members. Such was the intensity of persecution that on some occasions individual members may have been reluctant to identify themselves as Unification Church members out of fear of harassment or abuse, despite Rev. Moon's admonition that members always proudly acknowledge their membership. Members were sometimes fearful that if they admitted they were "Moonies," they would not be permitted to carry out their fundraising or witnessing activities, and in many instances this was precisely what happened. Unification Church members have often received discriminatory treatment simply by virtue of their Church membership.

One of the most frequently-cited allegations has to do with the so-called "front groups" of the Unification Church. It has been alleged by detractors of the Church that various organizations have been set up by members of the Church under different names so as to prevent the public from knowing that the Unification Church is involved.

This allegation is in itself rather misleading because it is the general practice of any organization that is affiliated with Rev. Moon or the Unification Church to say so in its literature. This may not have occurred in *every* instance in the past, but it has become a clear policy over the past several years.

Thus the question arises as to why bother creating a new organization at all if Church members are proud to acknowledge their affiliation with Rev. Moon and the Unificaton Church. The answer to this question is twofold. First of all, many projects have been set up in an effort to gather individuals from very diverse religious backgrounds for the purpose of creating joint enterprises dealing with mutual concerns in which the Unification Church would be but one of many participants. The vast majority of participants have no affiliation (nor desire to affiliate) with the Unification Church, yet they have a strong interest in the particular goals of the project or organization. Therefore, they are willing to participate in a joint non-denominational enterprise which will not force them to compromise their own beliefs. At the same time, projects such as the ecumenical conferences allow them to work towards accomplishing important goals in which all religions have a stake.

A second factor that may occasionally play a role is that the media have created such a twisted image of the Church that some of its efforts would possibly find outright rejection if presented solely as activities of the Unification Church. The anticultists have certainly been successful in grossly distorting the public image of the Unificaton Church and then using that controversial image to make allegations of deception whenever the Church tries to avoid that false image.[28]

Another concern has related to the names that have been chosen for these various organizations, particularly when they resemble existing organizations. This is often the result of inexperience in the organizational world by those Church members who are seeking to launch new projects.

A widely publicized example of the "deception" allegation was in Northern California where Church members had established an idealistic communal organization called "Creative Community Project" (CCP) during the early 1970s. That some of those who participated in various programs did not always know immediately of the affiliation with the Unification Church was not an issue during the early years because many people had never heard of Rev. Moon or cared about any affiliation, nor was there a nationally established Church at that time. It was only after a number of people had their faith broken through deprogramming that charges of "deception" emerged. Encouraged by the anti-cult movement, a number of apostates coined the phrase "heavenly deception" to describe this allegation.

In responding to this issue, Unification Church President Mose Durst writes:

> *Insofar as some of our zealous evangelists may have downplayed Rev. Moon in our earliest contacts in the past, such is now clearly and expressly against our policy and our instructions to members of the Church. In fact, after our introductory supper and lecture at evening programs across the country, the members who invite people to come up "to the land" for a seminar say "We will study the teachings of Rev. Moon."*[29]

Allegations of deception have historically been made against other religions. As stated earlier, Joseph Fichter acknowledged the many allegations of deception or "mental reservation" against the Jesuits.[30] Buddhists have likewise been accused of withholding "hidden teachings" and other types of trickery or deception.[31] Jewish organizations have accused Hebrew Christians or Messianic Jews of deception as well (see Chapter 1).[32]

Canadian religious studies professor Rodney Sawatsky, who is a member of the Mennonite faith, offers some useful insights into the tremendous persecution endured by the Unification Church. He asks:

> *Why is it that Unification members are being persecuted by deprogrammers, by some psychiatrists, by the media and even by the law? Are not all religions free to exist in America? Are these people any more brainwashed than Billy Graham converts, or Jesuit priests, or soldiers? It is very doubtful. The problem with the Moonies is that they are challenging the status quo. They are giving their whole lives to their faith. They are seeking perfection, the kingdom of God on earth. When the majority culture likes to think that "I'm OK, You're OK," that it is indeed building God's kingdom, Mennonites, Mormons and Moonies come along with an alternative proposal—and persecution begins.*[33]

Ultimately, there is a strong sense among Unificationists that the experience and training they receive in the Church, even through difficulties and persecution, is important in helping each one to become a better individual. Since the central, core teaching is that each person must love God and love one another, any progress that is made in that regard can only be of benefit, particularly for the couples' rearing of their own children. In other words, religious life is seen as an important training ground to mature each person's character in much the same tradition as the experience of religious ascetics of any other age or culture.

The Unification concept of self-sacrifice is comparable to that of Thomas Merton who writes: "The meaning of this sacrifice of ourselves is that we renounce the dominion of our own acts and of our own life and of our own death into the hands of God so that we do all things not for ourselves or according to our own will and our own desires, but for God, and according to His will."[34]

References

1. For a detailed explanation of Unification Church theology, please see the Divine Principle text as well as various summaries which are available to the public from HSA Publications, 4 West 43rd Street, New York NY, 10036. A useful commentary on the theology is provided by a variety of theologians in Herbert Richardson (ed.), *Ten Theologians Respond to the Unification Church* (New York: Rose of Sharon, 1981). See also Frank K. Flinn (ed.), *Hermeneutics and Horizons* (New York: Rose of Sharon, 1982); and Gordon Anderson, "The Unification Vision of the Kingdom of God on Earth" in M. Darrol Bryant and Donald W. Dayton (eds.), *The Coming Kingdom* (Barrytown, NY: International Religious Foundation, 1983).

2. Matt. 22: 37-40.

3. Richard Quebedeaux, "Korean Missionaries in America," in Henry O. Thompson (ed.), *Unity in Diversity* (New York: Rose of Sharon, 1984) x.

3*. Ibid.

4. See, for example, a description of the value of these conferences by sociologist Rodney Stark in the introduction to a book he edited, *Religious Movements: Genesis, Exodus, and Numbers* (New York: Paragon House, 1985) 4-5.

5. See, for example, Bowman L. Clarke & Eugene T. Long (eds.), *God and Temporality* (New York: Paragon House, 1984).

6. Quoted by Kurt Rudolph in "The Foundations of the History of Religions and Its Future Task," in Joseph M. Kitagarro (ed.), *The History of Religions* (New York: Macmillan, 1985) 115.

7. See essays by the diverse faculty members of the Unificaton Theological Seminary in Henry O. Thompson (ed.), *Unity in Diversity*, supra.

8. See *Introduction to the CAUSA Worldview* (New York: CAUSA Institute, 1985).

9. See the summary of these many projects by Rev. Moon in his testimony to the Senate Subcommittee on the Constitution oversight hearing on the state of religious liberty in America, June 26, 1984, supra, 160-169.

10. Martin Luther King, Jr., *Strength to Love* (Philadelphia: Fortress, 1963) 97-98.

11. Joseph Fichter, *The Holy Family of Father Moon,* supra, 69-70.

12. See generally, Richard Quebedeaux (ed.), *Lifestyle—Conversations with Members of the Unification Church* (New York: Rose of Sharon, 1982) The article "Engagement, Marriage and Children" by Hugh and Nora Spurgin and Arthur Eves may be particularly insightful.

13. James H. Grace, *Sex and Marriage in the Unification Movement, A Sociological Study* (New York: Edwin Mellen, 1984) vi.

14. Ibid., 267.

15. Ibid., 270. One of the main community service activities of Unification Church members is called "Home Church" whereby each member seeks to provide service to 360 homes in his or her neighborhood. See Joseph H. Fichter, "Home Church: Alternative Parish," in *Alternatives to American Mainline Churches* (New York: Rose of Sharon, 1983) 179.

16. Grace, ibid., 271-272.

17. Rev. Moon stated this clearly in an interview with theologian and author, Frederick Sontag. The interview is recorded in Sontag, *Sun Myung Moon and the Unification Church* (Nashville: Abingdon, 1977) 135, 143.

18. Joseph H. Fichter, "Marriage Family and Sun Myung Moon," *America,* Oct. 27, 1979, 1. Indeed, Rev. Moon emphasizes that members should love their families: "Since you joined this church I have always taught you to love your parents: I have never taught you to look at them as 'false parents' or to denounce them in any way." ("Perfection of Restoration by Indemnity through Human Responsibility," March 1, 1983).

19. Ibid.

20. *Day of Hope III* (Tarrytown: IOWC, 1981) 686-687. The reaction of many parents has been quite positive. for example, in 1976, hundreds of parents took the time to attend a national parents' seminar in New York City. Following the conference, more than 200 parents signed a proclamation which stated in part:

 "Our sons and daughters, through the teachings of the Unification Church, have developed a deep love for God, and for their fellow man and we are proud that they have decided to dedicate this time in their lives to help their communities and countries. They have found a direction for their lives and new hope for the future with a possibility of peace for this nation and the world. Participating in the Unification Church has developed the following character traits which we feel are entirely positive and desirable:

 *Increased consideration and awareness toward the value, uniqueness and feelings of others and especially of their personal families.

 *A strong sense of right coupled with a high moral code of ethics.

 *The self discipline to accomplish any task set before them. As the Bible states we must judge everything by its fruits. These fruits are young people who have dedicated their lives for the betterment of man, fulfilling God's will for world unity and peace, and accomplishing this seemingly impossible task through love and caring with the heart of God rather than with guns and violence. In conclusion, we are in full support of our sons and daughters and of the teaching of the Unification Church for its inspiration and new hope revitalizing the spirit of these precious young people. We believe that this group should be supported by all Americans if we want democracy to win over atheism, solid family unity to prevail over broken families, and strong courageous youth to prosper over corrupt and immoral youth." Ibid.

21. Ibid.

22. Ibid. See also "Here's New Twist: Mom understands Moonie Daughter," *Albuquerque Journal* (Albuquerque, NM), April 5, 1980.

23. This was predicted by Rev. Moon in an interview with Frederick Sontag in 1977. See Sontag, supra, 155.

24. Martin A. Larson and C. Stanley Lowell, *The Religious Empire* (Washington, DC: Luce, 1976) 65. Of course, these estimates do not include real estate owned by Catholics or Unificationists in their private capacity.

25. Ibid., 181.

26. Professor Richard Quebedeaux deals with a similar point when he writes: "Jonathan Wells, a Ph.D. student in religious studies at Yale, a veteran Berkeley radical—incarcerated for a year at Leavenworth for draft resistance—and a Unificationist, told his story in the *Yale Daily News* in 1978. His concluding remarks in that article sum up quite adequately the reasons why intelligent and idealistic white American young people are attracted and follow a 'slant eyed' Korean evangelist with a vision of the kingdom of heaven on earth: 'It's not easy to follow Rev. Moon. In the past four years, I've experienced enough verbal abuse, police harassment, and physical assault to make the time I spent at Leavenworth seem like a vacation. But it's often the case that the best way is not the easiest. When I went to prison, that seemed the best way to uphold high ideals in a messed-up world. I still have high ideals. the times have changed, but the dream has not diminished." Richard Quebedeaux, "Korean Missionaries to America," in

Henry O. Thompson (ed.), *Unity in Diversity,* (New York: Rose of Sharon, 1984) xxiii.

27. Editorial, *New Tomorrow,* (London, UK), May 1981, 5.

28. During a national conference of scholars and writers at the Graduate Theological Union in Berkeley, California in June, 1977, Harvey Cox refers to this reluctance as "simply a survival technique" for minority religious groups. See Rockefeller Foundation, *New Religious Movements in America* (The Rockefeller Foundation, 1979).

29. Durst, *To Bigotry, No Sanction,* 163-164.

30. Allegations of "deceptive practices to recruit naive teenagers and college students" have been made recently against the Catholic "Opus Dei" organization. See "A Church within the Church," *San Francisco Examiner* (San Francisco, California), June 1, 1986.

31. See Dr. P. Masefield, "The Muni and the Moonies," *Religion,* vol. 15, 1985, 143-160.

32. See also David Rausch, "Jews Against 'Messianic' Jews," in Herbert Richardson (ed.), *New Religions and Mental Health,* supra, 39.

33. Rodney Sawatsky, "Moonies, Mormons and Mennonites," in *A Time for Consideration,* supra, 37-38.

34. Thomas Merton, *No Man is an Island,* supra, 102.

CONCLUSION

Aside from a difference in lifestyle and the fact that established churches have a fear of losing members to the newer religions, what then is the threat that they pose to Western society? To take a religious perspective, the history of being persecuted is a sad, yet well-known tradition for prophets and the prophetic message. In fact, the historical role of the prophet is to shake people up. The Old Testament is filled with such stories, and the history of Christianity is no less a record of the prophetic message being misunderstood and often entirely rejected.

Unificationists believe that human beings are born with original sin, which translates into our "fallen" or "selfish" nature. It is to such "selfish" people that God has sought to send his message throughout the ages—from Noah to Abraham, from Elijah to Christ himself, and from St. Francis and Martin Luther to Martin Luther King and Sun Myung Moon.

It is always difficult to receive God's message because it usually means we have to change. If there is anything human beings cherish it is to be secure and comfortable in their situation, even if their lives are unfulfilled. People often accept a mundane existence, giving up on their childhood dreams because "Somewhere Over The Rainbow" is just a song. Thus, we build our lives around a set of values that may include God but we often fail to center totally on our Heavenly Father.

However, God is a living God who takes an intense and active interest in the lives of His children. He remains desperate for us to fully dwell with Him. Unfortunately, God does not have hands and feet, and the only voice He has is the voice of His messengers. But the messenger is often seen as a threat to the status quo in the world. He reminds us that a life of seeking after worldly pleasures will not bring us to the bosom of God. He challenges us to let go of our worldly cares and to follow after him. Jesus' words to his disciples ring in our ears, yet we somehow fail to believe that his words apply to us. Thus, we justify our worldly habits and ignore the prophetic message.

But there is one problem with the prophet—he is aggressive and he doesn't give up. He keeps shouting his message from the housetops and even the mountaintops. People seem to have only two choices: to come and heed the prophetic message and dramatically alter their lives, or to stone or crucify the prophet.

It is sad to say that much of history is a history of stoning the prophets, as St. Stephen so bravely lamented: "You stiff-necked people, uncircumcised in heart and ears, you always resist the Holy Spirit. As your fathers did, so do you. Which of the prophets did not your fathers persecute? And they killed those who announced beforehand the coming of the Righteous One, whom you have now betrayed and murdered, you who received the law as delivered by angels and did not keep it."[1]

Rev. Moon fits into the prophetic tradition. His speeches are filled with exhortations to follow the example of the prophets of the past. For instance, in a speech entitled "The Future of Christianity," he described Abraham's experience: "God called Abraham, the son of an idol-maker, and commanded him, 'Leave your home at once!' God does not allow for any compromise. God takes a position where evil can be totally denied. In no other way can good begin."[2] Rev. Moon went on to say: "God has said He will start a new history, in which no element of evil will remain. God demands complete response from man. Those who follow God's direction must begin from absolute denial of the evil world. That is why Jesus Christ taught: 'He who finds his life will lose it, and he who loses his life for my sake will find it.'"[3]

The vision of the Unification Church is a challenging one, a confronting one. As this book has explained, there are many historical parallels that can be drawn to the experience of the Unification Church. As this becomes more fully understood, it is hoped that the abuse and bigotry of the early years will fade and ultimately disappear. Yet, regardless of whether the Unification message is popular or unpopular, it will continue to offer its vision of a new world, the ideal world that God and mankind have yearned for throughout the ages. As Robert F. Kennedy often said:

Some men see things as they are
and say why.
I dream things that never were
and say why not.[4]

References

1. Acts 7: 51-53.

2. Sun Myung Moon, *Christianity in Crisis—New Hope* (Washington, DC: HSA-UWC, 1974) 83.

3. Ibid., quoting Matt. 10: 39.

4. Pierre Salinger, Edwin Guthman, Frank Mankiewicz and John Seigenthaler (eds.), *An Honorable Profession: A Tribute to Robert F. Kennedy* (New York: Doubleday, 1968) 3.

SELECTED BIBLIOGRAPHY

Ahlstrom, Sydney E. *A Religious History of the American People,* New Haven: Yale University Press, 1972

Allport, Gordon W. *The Nature of Prejudice,* Reading MA: Addison-Wesley, 1954.

Anderson, Gordon "The Unification Vision of the Kingdom of God on Earth", in M. Darrol Bryant and Donald W. Dayton, eds. *The Coming Kingdom,* Barrytown, NY: International Religious Foundation, 1983.

Bacon, Margaret H. *The Quiet Rebels,* New York: Basic Books, 1969.

Barker, Eileen *The Making of A Moonie,* New York: Basic Blackwell, 1984.

Beckford, James A. "'Brainwashing' and 'Deprogramming' in Britain: The Social Sources of Anti-Cult Sentiment", in David G. Bromley and James T. Richardson, eds. *The Brainwashing/Deprogramming Controversy: Sociological, Psychological, Legal and Historical Perspectives,* New York: Edwin Mellen, 1983.

Beckford, James A. "Through the Looking-Glass and out the Other Side: Withdrawal from Reverend Moon's Unification Church", *Archives des Sciences Sociales des Religion,* vol. 45, 1978, 95.

Berger, Herbert and Peter C. Hexel *Ursachen and Wirkungen gesellschaftlicher Verweigerung junger Munschen unter besonderer Berucksichtigung der "Jugendreligionen",* Vienna, 1981.

Billington, Ray *The Protestant Crusade 1800-1860,* Chicago: Quadrangle, 1938.

Boorstin, Daniel J. *The Image: A Guide to Pseudo-Events in America,* New York: Antheum, 1973.

Boothby, Lee "Government as an Instrument of Retribution for Private Resentments" in Dean Kelley, ed. *Government Intervention in Religious Affairs II,* New York: Pilgrim Press, 1986.

Bromley, David G. "Ted Patrick and The Development of Deprogramming,", presented at the 1985 Annual Meeting of the Society for the Scientific Study of Religion.

Bromley, David G. and Anson D. Shupe, Jr. "The Archetypal Cult: Conflict and the Social Construction of Deviance" in Gene J. James, ed. *The Family and the Unification Church,* New York: Rose of Sharon, 1983.

Bromley, David G. and James T. Richardson, eds. *The Brainwashing/Deprogramming Controversy: Sociological, Psychological, Legal, and Historical Perspectives,* New York: Edwin Mellen, 1983.

Bromley, David G. and Anson D. Shupe, Jr. *Strange Gods: The Great American Cult Scare,* Boston: Beacon Press 1981.

Bromley, David G. and Anson D. Shupe, Jr. *The New Vigilantes,* Beverly Hills: Sage, 1980.

Bromley, David. G. and Anson D. Shupe, Jr. "The Tnevnoc Cult", *Sociological Analysis,* 1979.

Bryant, M. Darrol and Herbert Richardson, eds. *A Time For Consideration: A Scholarly Appraisal of the Unification Church,* New York: Edwin Mellen, 1978.

Chorover, Stephen "Mental Health as a Social Weapon" in Herbert Richardson, ed. *New Religions and Mental Health,* New York: Edwin Mellen, 1980.

Cohn, Norman *Warrant for Genocide: The Myth of the Jewish World-Conspiracy and the Protocols of the Elders of Zion,* Chico, CA: Scholars Press, 1981.

Coleman, Lee *Psychiatry the Faithbreaker: How psychiatry is promoting bigotry in America,* Sacramento: Printing Dynamics, 1982.

Cox, Harvey "Deep Structures in the Study of New Religions", in Jacob Needleman and George Baker, eds. *Understanding the New Religions,* New York: Seabury, 1978.

Cox, Harvey Introduction to David G. Bromley and Anson D. Shupe, Jr. *Strange Gods: The Great American Cult Scare,* Boston: Beacon Press, 1981.

Cox, Harvey "Myths Sanctioning Religious Persecution" in M. Darrol Bryant and Herbert Richardson, eds. *A Time For Consideration,* New York: Edwin Mellen, 1978.

Davis, David Brion "Some Themes of Counter-Subversion: An Analysis of Anti-Masonic, Anti-Catholic, and Anti-Mormon Literature", *The Mississippi Valley Historical Review,* vol., XLVII, No. 2, September, 1960, 205.

DeMaria, Richard "A Psycho-Social Analysis of Religious Conversion." M. Darrol Bryant and Herbert Richardson, eds. *A Time For Consideration,* New York: Edwin Mellen Press, 1978

DeSocio, Walter G. "Protecting the Rights of Religious Cults", *Human Rights,* vol. 8, Number 3, 1979.

Durst, Mose *To Bigotry, No Sanction,* Chicago: Regnery Gateway, 1984.

Elkins, Chris *What Do You Say to A Moonie?,* Wheaton, IL: Tyndale House, 1981.

Ellwood, Robert "The Several Meanings of Cult", *Thought, Fordham University Quarterly,* vol. LXI, June, 1986.

Fichter, Joseph H. "Hammering the Heretics", *Witness,* vol. 66, No. 1, Jan. 1983.

Fichter, Joseph H. "Home Church: Alternative Parish", in Joseph H. Fichter, ed. *Alternatives to American Mainline Churches,* New York: Rose of Sharon Press, 1983.

Fichter, Joseph H. "Marriage, Family and Sun Myung Moon", *America,* Oct. 27, 1979.

Fichter, Joseph H. *The Holy Family of Father Moon,* Kansas City: Leaven Press, 1985.

Fichter, Joseph H. "Youth in Search of the Sacred", Bryan Wilson, ed. *The Social Impact of New Religious Movements,* New York: Rose of Sharon Press, 1981.

Flinn, Frank K. "Criminalizing Conversion: The Legislative Assault on New Religions *et al.*", in James Day and William Laufer, eds. *Crimes, Values and Religion,* Norwood, NJ: Ablex Publishing, 1986.

Flinn, Frank K. ed., *Hermeneutics and Horizons,* New York: Rose of Sharon, 1982.

Flowers, Ronald B. *Religion in Stange Times: The 1960's and 1970's,* Mercer University Press, 1984.

Fort, Joel "Mind Control: The What and How of Conversion and Indoctrination ('Brainwashing')" in H. Wang, ed. *Clinical Hypnosis in Medicine,* Chicago: Yearbook Medical Publishers, 1981.

Galanter, Marc "The 'Moonies', a Psychological Study", presented to 131st Annual Meeting of the American Psychiatric Assoc., Atlanta, GA, 1978.

Grace, James H. *Sex and Marriage in the Unification Movement, A Sociological Study,* New York: Edwin Mellen, 1984.

Grenier, Richard "The New Priesthood". Paper presented at Seventh World Media Conference, Tokyo, Japan, Nov. 19-22, 1984.

Gutman, Jeremiah S. "Extemporaneous Remarks", *Review of Law and Social Change,* vol. 9, 1980-1981, 11.

James, William *The Varieties of Religious Experience,* New York: Macmillan, 1961.

Johnson, Paul E. *Psychology of Religion,* Nashville: .Abingdon, 1959.

Katz, Samuel *Battleground,* New York: Bantam, 1973.

Kelley, Dean "Deprogramming and Religious Liberty", *Civil Liberties Review,* vol. 4, July/Aug. 1977,23

Kempis, Thomas a. *The Imitation of Christ,* New York: Penguin, 1952.

Kilbourne, Brock K. and James T. Richardson "Anti-Religion Bias in the Diagnostic and Statistical Manual [DSM] III: The Case of the Cults", presented to the Annual Meeting for the Scientific Study of Religion, Chicago, 1984.

Kilbourne, Brock K. and James T. Richardson "Cultphobia", *Thought, Fordham University Quarterly,* vol. LXI, June, 1986.

Kibourne, Brock K. and James T. Richardson "Psychotherapy and New Religions in a Pluralistic Society", *American Psychological Association,* vol. 39, 1984.

Kilbourne, Brock K. and James T. Richardson "Social Experimentation, Self-Process or Social Role", *The International Journal of Social Psychiatry,* vol. 31, 1985.

Kilbourne, Brock K. "The Conway and Siegelman Claims Against Religious Cults: An Assessment of Their Data", *Journal For the Scientific Study of Religion,* vol. 22, No. 4, Dec., 1983.

King, Martin Luther, Jr. *Strength to Love,* Philadelphia: Fortress, 1963.

Kung, Hans "Religion: The Final Taboo?" *Origins,* May 29, 1986.

Larson, Martin A. and C. Stanley Lowell *The Religious Empire,* Washington, DC: Luce, 1976.

LeMoult, John E. "Deprogramming Members of Religous Sects", *Fordham Law Review*, vol. 46, 1978, 599.

Lewis, James R. "'Information Disease' and the Legitimation of Religous Freedom", presented at the annual meeting of the Association for the Sociology of Religion, Aug. 25-27, 1985.

Lewis, James R. and David G. Bromley "The Cult Withdrawal Syndrome: A Case of Misattrition of Cause?" forthcoming in the *Journal for the Scientific Study of Religion,* Sept. 1987.

Lichter, S. Robert and Stanley Rothman "The Media Elite and American Value", Ethics and Public Policy Center, No. 38, April, 1982.

Lifton, Robert J. *Thought Reform and the Psychology of Totalism,* New York: Norton, 1961.

Littell, Franklin H. *The Origins of Sectarian Protestantism,* New York: Macmillan, 1964.

Lunde, Donald T. and Thomas E. Wilson "Brainwashing as a Defence to Criminal Liability: Patty Hearst Revisited", *Criminal Law Bulletin,* vol. 13, 1977,341.

Lunde, Donald T. and Henry A. Sigal "Use and Abuse of DSM-III in 'Cult' Litigation", forthcoming.

Matczak, Sebastian A. *Unificationism, A New Philosophy and Worldview,* New York: Learned Publications, 1982.

Mather, Cotton *On Witchcraft,* New York: Bell, 1974.

McGowan, Thomas "Conversion: a Theological View" in Herbert Richardson, ed. *New Relgions and Mental Health,* New York: Edwin Mellen, 1980.

McGowan, Thomas "Horace Bushnell and the Unification Movement: A Comparison of Theologies", in Herbert Richardson, ed. *Ten Theologians Respond to the Unification Church,* New York: Rose of Sharon, 1981.

Meerloo, Joost A.M. *The Rape of the Mind: The Psychology of Thought Control, Menticide, and Brainwashing,* Cleveland: World, 1956.

Melton, J. Gordon and Robert L. Moore *The Cult Experience,* New York: Pilgrim Press, 1982.

Merton, Thomas *No Man is An Island,* New York: Harvest/HBJ, 1955.

Miller, Donald E. "Deprogramming in Historical Perspective" in David G. Bromley and James T. Richardson, eds. *The Brainwashing/Deprogramming Controversy,* New York: Edwin Mellen, 1983.

Moon, Sun Myung *Christianity in Crisis - New Hope,* Washington, DC: HSA-UWC, 1974.

Needleman, Jacob and George Baker, eds. *Understanding the New Religions,* New York, Seabury, 1978.

New York University Law Review, note, "Conservatorships and Religious Cults: Diving A Theory of Free Exercise", vol. 53, 1978, 1247.

Niebuhr, Reinhold "Grace as Power in, and as Mercy towards, Man," in William E. Conn, ed. *Conversion,* New York: Alba House, 1978.

O'Gorman, Edith *Convent Life Unveiled,* London: Lile and Fawcett, circa 1881.

Outler, Albert C., ed. *John Wesley,* New York: Oxford University Press, 1964.

Pfeffer, Leo Brief Amicus Curiae for the Institute for the Study of American Religion, in support of petition for certiorari, in Herbert Richardson, ed. *Constitutional Issues in the Case of Reverend Moon,* New York: Edwin Mellen, 1984.

Pfeffer, Leo "Equal Protection For Unpopular Sects", *Review of Law and Social Change,* vol. 9, 1980-81, 9.

Powell, Jody *The Other Side of the Story,* New York: William Morrow, 1984.

Quebedeaux, Richard, ed. *Lifestyle - Conversations with Members of the Unification Church,* New York: Rose of Sharon, 1982.

Rausch, David "Jews Against 'Messianic' Jews", in Herbert Richardson, ed. *New Religions and Mental Health,* New York: Edwin Mellen, 1980.

Reich, Walter "Brainwashing, Psychiatry, and the Law", *Psychiatry,* vol. 39, Nov. 1976.

Richardson, Herbert, ed. *Constitutional Issues in the Case of Reverend Moon,* New York: Edwin Mellen, 1984.

Richardson, Herbert, ed. *New Religions and Mental Health,* New York: Edwin Mellen, 1980.

Richardson, James T. "Conversion, Brainwashing, and Deprogramming in New Religious Groups", presented to faculty of the Free University of Amsterdam, *Religieuze Bewegingen in Nederland,* May 1, 1981.

Richardson, James T. "Leaving and Labeling: Voluntary and Coerced Disaffiliation From Religious Social Movements", forthcoming in Kurt Lang, ed. *Research in Social Movements, Conflicts and Change,* vol. 9, Greenwich, CT: JAI Press, 1985.

Robbins, Thomas "'Uncivil Religions' and Religious Deprogrammings", *Thought, Fordham University Quarterly,* vol. LXI, June, 1986, 278.

Robbins, Thomas and Dick Anthony "Brainwashing and the Persecution of Cults", *Journal of Religion and Health,* vol. 19, No. 1, 1980.

Robbins, Thomas, William C. Shepherd and James McBride, eds. *Cults, Culture and the Law,* Chico, CA: Scholars Press, 1985.

Robbins, Thomas and Dick Anthony "New Religions, Families and 'Brainwashing'", *In Gods We Trust*, New Brunswick, NJ: Transaction, 1981.

Robbins, Thomas and Dick Anthony "Deprogramming, Brainwashing and the Medicalization of Deviant Religious Groups", *Social Problems*, vol. 29, 1982, 283.

Scheflin, Alan W. and Edward M. Option, Jr. *The Mind Manipulators*, New York: Paddington Press, 1978.

Schein, Edgar *Coercive Persuasion: A Socio-Psychological Analysis of the "Brainwashing" of American Civilian Prisoners by the Chinese Communists*, New York: North, 1961.

Sciarrino, Alfred J. "'Free Exercise' Footsteps in the Defamation Forest: Are 'New Religions' Lost?", *The American Journal of Trial Advocacy*, vol. 7, 1984, 59-60.

Sciarrino, Alfred J. "United States v. Sun Myung Moon: Precedent for Tax Fraud Prosecution of Local Pastors", *Southern Illinois University Law Journal*, 1984, 237.

Shapiro, Robert N. "Indoctrination, Personhood, and Religious Beliefs", in Thomas Robbins, William C. Shepherd and James McBride, eds. *Cults, Culture, and the Law*, Chico, CA: Scholars Press, 1985.

Shapiro, Robert N. "Mind Control or Intensity of Faith: The Constitutional Protection of Religious Beliefs", *Harvard Civil Liberties Review*, vol. 13, 1978, 751.

Shapiro, Robert N. "Of Robots, Persons, and the Protection of Religious Beliefs", *Southern Calfifornia Law Review*, vol. 56, 1983, 1277.

Shepherd, William C. *To Secure the Blessings of Liberty*, New York: Crossroad Publishing, 1985.

Shupe, Anson D. and David G. Bromley "Witches, Moonies, and Accusations of Evil" in Thomas Robbins and Dick

Anthony, eds. *In Gods We Trust: New Patterns of Religious Pluralism in America,* New York: Transaction Books, 1981.

Siegel, Terri "Deprogramming Religious Cultists", *Loyola of Los Angeles Review,* vol. 11, 1978,812.

Solomon, Trudy "Integrating the 'Moonie' Experience: A Survey of Ex-Members of the Unification Church", in Thomas Robbins and Dick Anthony, eds. *In Gods We Trust,* New Brunswick, NJ: Transaction, 1981.

Solomon, Trudy "Programming and Deprogramming, the Moonies: Social Psychology Applied", in David Bromley and James T. Richardson, eds. *The Brainwashing/Deprogramming Controversy,* New York: Edwin Mellen, 1983.

Sontag, Frederick *Sun Myung Moon and the Unification Church,* Nashville: Abingdon, 1977.

Stark, Rodney, ed. *Religious Movements: Genesis, Exodus, and Numbers,* New York: Paragon House, 1985.

Stokes, Anson Phelps and Leo Pfeffer *Church and State in the United States,* New York: Harper & Row, 1964.

Streiker, Lowell *Mind-Bending,* New York: Doubleday, 1984.

Szasz, Thomas "Some Call It Brainwashing", *The New Republic,* March 6, 1976.

Testa, Bart, "It Would Have Been Nice To Hear From You...On fifth estate's 'Moonstruck'" in M. Darrol Bryant and Herbert Richardson, eds. *A Time For Consideration,* New York: Edwin Mellen, 1978.

Testa, Bart "Making Crime Seem Natural: The Press and Deprogramming" in M. Darrol Bryant and Herbert Richardson, eds. *A Time For Consideration,* New York: Edwin Mellen, 1978.

Thompson, Henry O., ed. *Unity in Diversity,* New York: Rose of Sharon, 1984.

Tillett, Gregory "The Moonies, The Media and Religious Persecution", (Unpublished), 1982.

Tillich, Paul *The Shaking of the Foundations,* New York: Scribner, 1948.

Van Driel, Barend and James T. Richardson "Cult Versus Sect - Categorization of New Religious Movements in the American Print Media", presented for the Annual Meeing of the Association for the Sociology of Religion, New York, NY, Aug. 1986.

Wallis, Roy *Sectarianism: Analysis of Religious and Non-Religious Sects,* London: Peter Owen, 1975.

Ward, Maria *Female Life Among the Mormons,* New York: J.C. Derby, 1855.

Wood, James E. Jr., "New Religions and the First Amendment", *Journal of Church and State,* vol. 24, 1982.

Wright, Stuart A. "Post-Involvement Attitudes of Voluntary Defectors From Controversial New Religious Movements," *Journal for the Scientific Study of Religion,* vol. 23, No. 2, 172.

BIBLIOGRAPHY OF LEGAL CITATIONS

Colombrito v. Kelly, 764 F.2d 122 (2nd Cir. 1985).

Cooper v. Molko, 512 F. Supp. 563 (N.D. Cal. 1981).

Eilers v. Coy, 582 F. Supp. 1093 (E.D. Minn. 1984).

Heffron v. ISCKON, 452 U.S. 640 (1981).

Holy Spirit Association for the Unification of World Christianity v.Michigan Dept. of Treasury, 131 Mich. App. 743 (1984).

Holy Spirit Association for the Unification of World Christianity v. Tax Commission of the City of New York, 55. N.Y. 2d 512 (1982).

Katz v. Superior Court, 73 Cal. App. 3d 952 (1977).

Larson v. Valente, 456 U.S. 228 (1982).

Lewis v. Holy Spirit Association, 589 F. Supp. 10 (D. Mass. 1983).

Love v. Mayor, City of Cheyenne, 448 F. Supp. 128. (D.WY. 1978).

McMurdie v. Doutt, 468 F. Supp. 766 (N.D. Ohio 1979).

Meroni v. Holy Spirit Association, App. Div. (2nd Dept.) Supreme Court of New York, Sept. 2, 1986.

Molko and Leal v. Holy Spirit Association for The Unification of World Chrisitianity, 179 Cal. App. 3d 450 (1986).

People v. Murphy, Affidavit of Sept. 29, 1976, submitted to the Supreme Court of New York, #2012-76.

Rankin v. Howard, 633 F.2d 844 (9th Cir. 1980) *cert. denied,* 451 U.S. 939 (1981).

Schuppin v. Unification Church, 435 F. Supp. 603 (D. VT. 1977).

Taylor v. Gilmartin, 686 F.2d 1346 (10th Cir. 1982) *cert. denied,* 459 U.S. 1147 (1983).

Troyer v. Town of Babylon, 483 F. Supp. 1135 (E.D.N.Y. 1980).

Turner v. Unification Church, 473 F. Supp. 367 (D.R.I. 1978).

Unification Church v. Immigration and Naturalization Service, 547 F. Supp. 623 (D.D.C. 1982).

United States v. Ballard, 322 U.S. 78 (1944).

United States v. Seeger, 380 U.S., 163 (1965).

United States v. Sun Myung Moon brief for the National Council of Churches *et al,* in support of petition for *certiorari* to the United States Supreme Court.

United States v. Sun Myung Moon brief for the Catholic League for Religious and Civil Rights, in support of petition for *certiorari* to the United States Supreme Court.

Ward v. Connor, 657 F.2d 45 (4th Cir. 1981) *cert. denied, sub nom. Mandelkorn v. Ward,* 455 U.S. 907 (1982).

Welsh v. United States, 398 U.S., 333 (1970).

Wollersheim v. Church of Scientology, Superior Court of California, Los Angeles County, No. C 332027, July 22, 1986.

INDEX

The Edwin Mellen Press publishes scholarly books in all academic disciplines. We invite manuscript proposals. Write for our free "How to Publish" brochure. Write the Editor, The Edwin Mellen Press, 240 Portage Road, Lewiston, New York, 14092, or phone (716) 754-2266.

THE LIBRARY
ST. MARY'S COLLEGE OF MARYLAND
ST. MARY'S CITY, MARYLAND 20686

Also published by the Edwin Mellen Press:

SYMPOSIUM SERIES

1. Jurgen Moltman *et al.*, **Religion and Political Society**
2. James Grace, editor, **God, Sex, and the Social Project: The Glassboro Papers on Religion and Human Sexuality**
3. M. Darrol Bryant and Herbert Richardson, editors, **A Time for Consideration: A Scholarly Appraisal of the Unification Church**
4. Donald G. Jones, editor, **Private and Public Ethics: Tensions Between Conscience and Institutional Responsibility**
5. Herbert Richardson, editor, **New Religions and Mental Health: Understanding the Issues**
6. Sheila Greeve Davaney, editor, **Feminism and Process Thought: The Harvard Divinity School/Claremont Center for Process Studies Symposium Papers**
7. International Movement, A.T.D./Fourth World, **Children of Our Time: The Children of the Fourth World**
8. Jenny Hammett, **Woman's Transformations: A Psychological Theology**
9. S. Daniel Breslauer, **A New Jewish Ethics**
10. Darrell J. Fasching, editor, **The Jewish People in Christian Preaching**
11. Henry Vander Goot, **Interpreting the Bible in Theology and the Church**
12. Everett Ferguson, **Demonology of the Early Christian World**
13. Marcia Sachs Littell, editor, **Holocaust Education: A Resource Book for Teachers and Professional Leaders**
14. Char Miller, editor, **Missions and Missionaries in the Pacific**
15. John S. Peale, **Biblical History as the Quest for Maturity**
16. Joseph A. Buijs, editor, **Christian Marriage Today: Growth or Breakdown ?**
17. Michael Oppenheim, **What Does Revelation Mean for the Modern Jew?**
18. Carl F. H. Henry, **Conversations with Carl Henry: Christianity for Today**
19. John T. Biermans, **The Odyssey of New Religious Movements: Persecution, Struggle, Legitimation; A Case Study of the Unification Church**